Finding Our Way

Practical Solutions for Creating
a Supportive Home and
Community for the
Asperger Syndrome Family

Finding Our Way

Practical Solutions for Creating a Supportive Home and Community for the Asperger Syndrome Family

Kristi Sakai

Foreword
Brenda Smith Myles

JAFFREY PUBLIC LIBRARY

A͟PC

Autism Asperger Publishing Co.
P.O. Box 23173
Shawnee Mission, Kansas 66283-0173
www.asperger.net

© 2005 by Autism Asperger Publishing Co.
P.O. Box 23173
Shawnee Mission, Kansas 66283-0173
www.asperger.net

Publisher's Cataloging-in-Publication
(Provided by Quality Books, Inc.)

Sakai, Kristi.
    Finding our way : practical solutions for creating a supportive home and community for the Asperger syndrome family / Kristi Sakai ; foreword, Brenda Smith Myles
    p. cm.
    Includes bibliographical references.
    ISBN 1-931282-76-5
    LCCN 2005926834

    1. Asperger's syndrome. 2. Asperger's syndrome—Patients—Family relationships. 3. Asperger's syndrome—Social aspects. I. Title.

RJ506.A9S35 2005   362.196'858832
                         QBI05-700179

This book is designed in American Typewriter and Helvetica Neue.

Printed in the United States of America

Dedication

Nobuo, thank you for your love and acceptance, and for trusting me even when it sounds like another nutty idea.

Tom, Kito and Kaede, thank you for the gift of being yourselves. I honor you. I am always, first and foremost, your Mama.
–KS

When we were kids, my older brother used to tease me, "Before you were born God said, 'Anyone who wants brains, get in line,' but you thought He said, 'trains' and replied, 'No thanks, I don't want any.'"

Maybe it was more like this, "If you want beautiful, creative children who will laugh loudly, walk in circles, fill your house with Legos, but won't eat vegetables, get in line."

In my haste I didn't listen to the part about, "They'll also throw themselves on the floor sobbing at the grocery store, they'll never sleep, you'll have to use a shovel to pick up the collectable cards in their rooms and your free time will largely be spent attending heated meetings fighting for services for them."

Maybe I was talking and missed it, or maybe I thought there was a buffet, so I greedily got in line three times.

Acknowledgments

Thank You to My Community of Support!

To my editor, Kirsten McBride, for her clarity, steady hand with a red pencil and skillful ability to perform literary liposuction. You have graciously (and patiently!) led me through this process. My heartfelt thanks.

Brenda Myles, for helping me *see* my kids through eyes of understanding and recognize the beauty of who they are. Thank you for sharing the dream of giving parents tools so they can believe in themselves and be effective advocates for their children.

Joe Steiner, MS, PA, for his knowledge about behavior management and reward systems. And for telling me, "What others think of you is none of your business." Joe, words cannot express my deepest gratitude for your insight, wisdom and guidance.

Sue Scott and Amy Metzger, who have been here since the beginning. Our years of conversation and shared journey through mothering our unique children laid the foundation for this book.

Also:

Lori Stevens and Tom Hagg; Jennifer Sottolano; Jill Scott-Hinkle; Ronda Schelvan; Elizabeth Merritt; Beverly Caswell; and "Jake" and her trusty sidekick, Annie Carwile.

Tami Walters and the staff at Mighty Oaks Children's Therapy Center, including Brad Cox, Camille Juntunen, D. Alexandra Foss. Your dedication to children of all abilities in our community inspires me.

Keith "Boss" Myles and all the staff at the Autism Asperger Publishing Company. Also to Vivian Strand for her wonderful illustrations.

Central Linn Elementary School, especially Linda Hoyer, Jan Sansom, Dave Bolin and "Secretary Sue," who knows my voice even before I say who I am.

Foreword

Kristi Sakai is my friend. I have only a few friends and don't use the term lightly. I don't recall how we met. She probably sent me an email asking me about Asperger Syndrome or requesting advice for herself or her children's teacher. Knowing Kristi, my response was probably a well-deserved accolade. Kristi knows what she is doing and is a strong advocate for her three children with Asperger Syndrome.

We corresponded via email for several years and a friendship developed – it is interesting how today's technology helps us foster relationships with people we have not physically met. Kristi's emails made me think, laugh and respect her unique way of understanding children and youth with Asperger Syndrome.

This book was supposed to be a collaborative venture. Kristi and I outlined the book and decided who was to write each chapter. We also planned a date to meet at my house to put the final touches on the book. I had wanted to write a "practical solutions for the home" book for quite some time and thought that she and I would do a marvelous job together. Periodically, I received emails from Kristi with notes, paragraphs or pages she had written. Everything she sent was wonderful. Kristi also asked about my progress on the book and I told her that I was making some progress. I can't recall if I defined what "making some progress" meant – it means that I am in the thinking stage and have not put pencil to paper (or fingers to keyboard). I am a last-minute writer – it is not unusual for me to wait until a week or two before a deadline before writing.

Somewhere in the "making some progress" stage, I realized that I could not write the book. I did not understand the parent perspective first-hand and my information would not be "real." I waited to tell Kristi this until we met face-to-face. She, of course, protested that she couldn't write the book alone. I produced the one hundred or so pages she had sent me and told her that she already had! In fact, she had written one of the best books on Asperger Syndrome I have had the opportunity to read. This book is marvelous; a gift to families of children and youth with Asperger Syndrome.

Kristi and I believe that parents are the experts on their children. Mothers and fathers navigate their children through the complexities of life events, helping them to become independent and self-determined adults. Even in the best circumstances, parenting is challenging. When you have a child with Asperger Syndrome, the challenge is intensified. You become navigator, interpreter, advocate, the safe harbor in a storm – the roles are endless and there isn't enough time in the day to accomplish everything that needs to be done. Along with these challenges are the gifts that children give to their parents – unique perspectives, respect for subtle things that we might not notice, love for solitude, overwhelming love, and a sense of social justice, just to name a few.

While we recognize that parents are the experts on their child, we have noticed that many parents feel alone and sometimes doubt themselves when they have to explain why their child does things in certain ways or feel somewhat defensive (and justifiably so) when questioned about the necessity of strategies and interventions they use at home and in the community with their children. Hopefully, this marvelous book will help validate what you know about your child and what you do to make life comfortable and predictable. I know you will enjoy Kristi's information, perspective, humor and good advice! This book is truly a gift to us all!

> – Brenda Smith Myles, Ph.D., is an associate professor at the University of Kansas, who writes and speaks internationally on Asperger Syndrome and autism

A Few Notes About Terminology

Throughout the book the author refers to Asperger Syndrome (AS), autism spectrum disorders (ASD) and autism interchangeably.

The AS child is referred to as "he" in order to simplify things. The sibling of the AS child is always "she." The term "neurotypical" or "NT" is used to describe a typically developing child.

The goal of this book is to support families. We recognize and celebrate that families are diverse and made up of all variations of color, culture, religion and size. Although the author makes reference to the nuclear two-parent family, it is only an example based on her personal experience. Asperger Parents are parents regardless of gender or biological link. It boils down to a simple question: In all the world, are you the person who loves this child best, fights for him the hardest and dreams of a healthy and happy future for him? If so, then you are the parent, and that's all that matters; this book is for YOU.

The principles and tools presented in this book are almost universally applicable to all families, or at least the hope is that everyone can find something useful for his or her own unique family. Think of it as a "potluck," take what works for you and leave the rest for somebody else (or the second trip through the line!).

If you have questions or comments for the author, you may email her at: AspergerSyndromeHome@hotmail.com

Table of Contents

Chapter 3

Chapter 4

Chapter 5

Chapter 6

Introduction

Before our oldest son, Tom, was diagnosed at age 8, we'd never heard of Asperger Syndrome, yet it had affected almost every aspect of our family life. We were loving, attentive parents, but in spite of our efforts, our child's behavior was uncontrollable at times, and we struggled with self-doubts. We tried our best, but we were flying blind, not knowing that Asperger Syndrome was the underlying issue. Embarrassment and oversensitivity to judgment over our son's behavior often led us astray, and although it didn't feel right, sometimes we caved in to pressure to conform to more rigid forms of parenting. When these "helpful" suggestions didn't work either, some people implied, and others said outright, it wasn't the system of parenting that was failing – it was us.

An Asperger Parent Is ...

Even when we'd accidentally hit on something that worked well, we often received such harsh judgment and criticism from others that we further doubted our instincts. For example, sending our child to the highly recommended "time-out" alone was not even possible, much less effective. But when we removed him to a quiet location, stayed with him and soothed him with our comforting presence, he would calm down and be more cooperative. This was seen as "spoiling" him. We felt as though nothing we did was right.

Others meant well. We meant well. But without understanding the root of our child's puzzling behaviors, how could we truly know what he needed, much less meet those needs? Diagnosis was the key that began equipping us with the right tools for understanding. Once we learned the underlying causes of the behavior, it all began to make sense. We also realized the many ways we had completely blown it. We cringed as we remembered the moments when we had refused to be flexible when our child desperately needed that, insisting that he conform to some arbitrary standard set by others. But equally important and heartening, we also saw with clarity the many things we'd been right about after all. We were right to listen to our son's cues, to pay attention to how he reacted in certain situations, and make adjustments accordingly.

PATIENCE IS A VIRTUE!

Part Saint

Through this process we realized we'd been holding ourselves captive to others' expectations of how children should be raised, instead of what worked best for OUR family. We figured this out just in the nick of time because after Tom was diagnosed, our second son, Kito, and our daughter, Kaede, were also diagnosed with autism spectrum disorder/Asperger Syndrome.

Things have improved in the last five years, but it wasn't until I sat down and made a comparison that I was able to see how clearly the tools we've been implementing changed our lives significantly for the better.

Then ...

1. Our child was usually fine unless we went out. Then he'd have a meltdown. We couldn't understand why.

2. Terrible twos turned into terrible threes and fours. Others' looks became judgmental; people began to voice criticism. We were embarrassed and worried we were "bad" parents.

3. Our child didn't sleep. Neither did we!

4. We lived in constant wonder that an itchy shirt could cause so much trouble.

5. Our child screamed as if he was dying when we washed or cut his hair, when we helped him brush his teeth or cut his nails.

6. Mealtime was a battleground, We worried our child would waste away as he clamped his mouth shut and refused to eat all but a few consistent items.

7. Social situations were often disastrous. We almost always left with our child crying. People didn't invite us back. Our family began to withdraw from the outside world.

8. When we consulted doctors, psychologists, and even an evaluation center, no one could tell us what was "wrong" with our child. They just gave us more parenting advice that didn't help. In other words, it was our fault.

9. I read every parenting book I could lay my hands on; nothing worked well (or at all!) for our child.

10. We isolated ourselves in self-protection because we didn't have enough of the right kind of support for our family.

Now ...

1. Meltdowns still occur sometimes when we go out, but they are less frequent because we know how to help our children. We use priming so they know what to expect, predictions so they'll be prepared for disappointments, and know to keep outings short.

2. People still react the same way to our children's public meltdowns, but the difference is that even if we are struggling, we know we are meeting their needs appropriately. We know we aren't "bad" parents.

3. A consistent countdown routine, a picture schedule, an appropriate sensory diet and medication have resulted in better sleep for everyone.

4. Now that we understand the sensory issue for people with AS, we realize that in our family anything but cotton feels itchy. All tags are automatically removed. Any uncomfortable item of clothing is given away to someone else.

5. Learning self-regulation skills in occupational therapy has helped us and our kids survive grooming sessions. Also, we provide rewards, which motivates cooperation.

6. We pick our battles. No more food wars. We give vitamins to cover all the bases.

7. Our children are better able to tolerate some social situations. We prepare them with tools such as priming and predicting, we are aware of triggers and keep it short to ensure success. Plus, we have wonderful friends who understand our family, so we DO get invited back!

8. The correct diagnosis has been key to understanding our children and helping them.

9. I read books about Asperger Syndrome and finally found things that work!

10. We realized we needed other people in our lives: occupational and speech therapists, special education teachers, autism specialists, educational assistants, psychiatrists, psychologists, advocates, respite providers and friends. We have built a community of support.

We see our kids with new eyes of understanding and have developed skills to deal with their sensory and behavior issues. We've adopted a lifestyle that takes into consideration *their* specific needs as children with Asperger Syndrome and *our* needs as their parents. Given the following diagnostic criteria for Asperger Syndrome from the *Diagnostic and Statistical Manual – 4th Edition, Text Revision* (American Psychiatric Association, 2000), let us now set the stage for the remainder of this book by briefly looking at those characteristics of this neurological disorder that most impact the entire family.

Diagnostic Criteria for Asperger's Disorder (299.80): Diagnostic and Statistical Manual of Mental Disorders – Fourth Edition, Text Revision

A. Qualitative impairment in social interaction, as manifested by at least two of the following:
   (1) marked impairment in the use of multiple nonverbal behaviors such as eye-to-eye gaze, facial expression, body postures, and gestures to regulate social interaction
   (2) failure to develop peer relationships appropriate to developmental level
   (3) a lack of spontaneous seeking to share enjoyment, interests, or achievements with other people (e.g., by a lack of showing, bringing, or pointing out objects of interest to other people)
   (4) lack of social or emotional reciprocity

B. Restricted repetitive and stereotyped patterns of behavior, interests, and activities, as manifested by at least one of the following:
   (1) encompassing preoccupation with one or more stereotyped and restricted patterns of interest that is abnormal either in intensity or focus
   (2) apparently inflexible adherence to specific, nonfunctional routines or rituals
   (3) stereotyped and repetitive motor mannerisms (e.g., hand or finger flapping or twisting, or complex whole-body movements)
   (4) persistent preoccupation with parts of objects

C. The disturbance causes clinically significant impairment in social, occupational, or other important areas of functioning.

D. There is no clinically significant delay in language (e.g., single words used by age 2 years, communicative phrases used by 3 years).

E. There is no clinically significant delay in cognitive development or in the development of age-appropriate self-help skills, adaptive behavior (other than in social interaction), and curiosity about the environment in childhood.

F. Criteria are not met for another specific Pervasive Developmental Disorder or Schizophrenia.

Tools for Understanding the Characteristics of Asperger Syndrome That Impact the Family

Your child isn't moving through the world in an Asperger Syndrome bubble, everyone in his life is touched by it, especially his family. The diagnosis is the key, but once we enter the AS world, it's as if we need a translator who can explain our child's unusual behavior. What *is* going on? We won't touch on every aspect of Asperger Syndrome, but here's a brief overview to highlight how your child's AS may affect your family's daily life.

Sensory

The AS child is often oversensitive to smell, taste, touch, visual and auditory input, and has difficulties with other sensory issues, such as vestibular (balance) and proprioception (body awareness). Sensory issues can directly interfere with the smooth flow of family life in a multitude of ways, as illustrated below.

Smell. The AS child can have a meltdown seemingly out of the blue. He might have been set off by something as simple as a lady in a store whose perfume was too liberally applied. He may refuse to go to places he says smell "bad." He might be loud and expressive about his distaste, saying, "It STINKS!" This can embarrass parents.

Taste. He may be a picky eater. This can lead to conflicts at dinnertime and frustrated parents who worry about his diet. It can cause problems at family gatherings, especially when there isn't anything he will eat. When this occurs under the watchful eyes of extended family, they may express concern … or criticism. This, plus other behavior issues, can cause the AS Family to forego family holidays.

Touch. He might react negatively or refuse to wear all but a certain kind of clothing. He might have a meltdown if his shoes are uncomfortable. This is frustrating for parents who are just trying to find SOMETHING he will wear. He might be sensitive to the touch of others. In some cases, Mom might not be able to kiss him goodnight, or he may pull away when hugged. This is painful for the mother who wants to shower her child with loving affection and feels rejected.

Visual input. While the AS child is highly attentive to some things, these aren't always the things that he needs to attend to at a given time. He may be distracted and unable to find things he needs right under his nose, such a schoolbook. This means parents are constantly having to drop what they are doing to find lost items. Also, when going out, he might be easily OVERstimulated by too much visual input, feel overwhelmed and melt down. Parents often choose the lesser of two evils, and stay home out of sheer desperation, isolating their family.

Auditory. The AS child often has hypersensitive hearing. What is merely noisy to other people can be tortuously painful to his sharp ears. As a result, the noise of a crowd – a birthday part or a baseball game – may be too much to endure. For some, even the sound of certain people's voices can grate on their nerves and lead to meltdowns. For these reasons, the family may find it too difficult to take the child out to community activities they formerly enjoyed. Other children with AS, on the other hand, may have adapted by being able to completely tune out loud noises and voices. The child may reside in his own little world, failing to respond when spoken to. This can cause another kind of frustration for parents. It can even cause safety concerns when the child doesn't "hear" an urgent command from a frightened parent trying to warn of impending danger.

Vestibular (balance). He may feel dizzy or unsure when tipping his head back, which may make him "reluctant" to lean back to wash his hair. This can lead to bath time battles.

Proprioception (body awareness). The AS child may have difficulty understanding where his body starts and the world around him ends. He appears clumsy; he bumps into furniture and people, he accidentally breaks things. His parents are torn between worry that he will seriously injure himself, and annoyance at the sheer number of broken items they've had to replace.

All of these sensory issues are real; our AS kids aren't making it up. Working with a skilled occupational therapist can often help them become more flexible, address their specific needs, as well as a multitude of other issues such as fine- and gross-motor skills.

Does the entire world revolve around your child's needs? Of course not. It's about striking a balance between needs and long-term well-being for the entire family. We'll talk about that more throughout the book.

Behavior

Children with Asperger Syndrome don't carry any obvious outward physical appearance commonly associated with other neurological or physical disabilities. They generally "look" like every other kid, which is why we often hear the comment, "You can't even tell." The only thing people can "see" is the behavior. Children with Asperger Syndrome often display behaviors that to the outside world can appear anywhere from annoying to naughty, or at the very least, odd. Here are just a few examples.

Special interest. Most individuals with AS have a "special interest," a bordering-on-obsessive focus on a hobby, collection or topic. For kids it is often cards or toys with a certain theme, but it can be anything – even something as seemingly strange as washing machines! They may talk about their special interest incessantly, assuming that since it is so fascinating to them, everyone else must surely enjoy hearing about it as well. Hearing about it is the least of the associated inconveniences for parents; they may be constantly pestered into purchasing materials or toys associated with this interest. It can be wearing on the wallet, as well as frustrating when you finally find the "right" item to purchase and you're hardly out of the store before the child begins obsessing about the next item for his collection. Not to mention the purely practical matter of where on earth to put all these things.

Charming and not-so-charming quirks. Many people with AS display several common mannerisms, such as hand flapping, spinning, twirling or rocking. These are occasionally annoying to parents, but are relatively benign. Some of these mannerisms are ingenious ways of self-management; that is, a way to release stress, a coping mechanism. Others are more frightening to parents and onlookers such as head banging, which can occur during times of extreme stress. Such behavior is strange to witness if you don't understand what is happening, and painful for parents to experience.

Lack of eye contact. There are various reasons why kids with Asperger Syndrome do not make what we would view as typical eye contact. It can be lack of awareness or lack of desire to make that connection. Often it is reported that they struggle with attention, and feel they can listen better if they don't have to also concentrate on the visual input. Parents say, "Look at me when I'm talking to you, and pay attention!" Couple the apparent lack of eye contact with the child not giving a verbal response to your question, and it is easy to assume that the kid is just ignoring you. This can cause frustration and lead to impatience on the part of adults, upping the stress level for everyone.

Meltdowns and tantrums. You see a child throwing a fit and automatically assume that's a misbehaving child. End of story. Or is it? Our kids may react with crying, sobbing and literally throwing themselves on the floor when they have hit their limit, whether it's from sensory overload, frustration at not being able to communicate their needs or a host of other things. It *seems* to come on without warning and often happens in public when the poor kid is stretched as far as he can go and then snaps. Parents and siblings may cringe with embarrassment as they feel the judging eyes of others; they may also struggle with their own feelings of confusion and helplessness over what is happening. On top of that, it's exhausting to deal with such outbursts. Parents are always waiting for "the other shoe to drop," particularly if they don't understand that there is an antecedent to these rages; there is always an underlying cause that triggers them. Finally, every meltdown highlights a parent's worry over what will happen to the child in the future. We will talk more about meltdowns in Chapter 2.

Social Skills

Children with Asperger Syndrome face a mountain of social challenges, and therefore so do their families. All of the above issues are intertwined within the child, making them difficult to sort out. Even with proper diagnosis, it takes time to figure out what the child's specific issues are, much less how to deal with them. Parents may feel assaulted on all fronts: from the child and his behavior, from the judgment they feel from others. They may withdraw socially because they are overwhelmed by the child's behaviors and the expected rain of judgment falling down on them in the wake of a behavior issue.

Picture the following scene, followed by the explanation of the root causes of the various problems this family encounters.

No Walk in the Park

The Jones Family went to a community potluck at the park with their son, Trevor, who has Asperger Syndrome – but they aren't yet aware of it. The adults are gathered in one area talking and laughing, while the children are playing on the equipment lightly supervised from a short distance.

Trevor is having trouble getting along with his peers and keeps running to his mom and dad. Upset, he says, "They won't listen to me!" Trevor wants the other kids to stand still and listen to him talk about Pokémon. But the other kids want to run and play on the jungle gym. At first they try to include him, but eventually they are either too distracted by their own fun, or actually reject him because they think he's "weird." They climb up to the top of the jungle gym, but Trevor is afraid to go that high. When Trevor comes crying to his mom once more, one of the other mothers says loftily, "You have to just let kids work that stuff out on their own." His mom feels conflicted, and sends him off to play again.

Trevor's family stays despite their son's increasing agitation, optimistically hoping he'll settle down. His dad says, "Hang in there, buddy! Just a few more minutes and we can eat lunch and have dessert!" Trevor passes the dessert table and sees his favorite kind of pie. He pulls himself together to wait. The time finally arrives, and everyone lines up, paper plates in hand. It is loud, and in such close proximity to so many people, there is some bumping, and when Trevor accidentally loses his balance and falls hard into the lady ahead of him, she gives his parents a scowl. When it's finally Trevor's turn to get to the table, both he and his parents are dismayed to see an array of salads and casseroles. They finally find one or two items that he will eat and move to the dessert table. Trevor has been anticipating getting a piece of his favorite pie. But it's already gone. That is the straw that breaks the proverbial camel's back. He throws himself to the ground, wailing.

Trevor's parents are embarrassed, with everyone looking at them. They cajole, scold, threaten and try to bribe their son to stop, but nothing helps. A nice lady steps forward and tries to help by promising Trevor that next time she'll bring another pie. Rather than being comforted by her promise, Trevor merely screams in her face. She walks away looking scandalized while his parents profusely apologize. Mom says tearfully to her husband, "Let's just go!" Dad gathers up their things and the two of them half carry, half drag their sobbing son out to the car. On the way home the parents express frustration and disappointment to each other and decide that they won't be going to the next community potluck.

Interpretation: Seeing It Through Eyes of Understanding

It looks like Trevor is a brat and that he has bad parents. But is that the case? Absolutely not! Trevor has loving parents who wanted to enjoy a day out in the community with their son, but it all fell apart for them. To their untrained eyes, none of it makes sense – they do not understand why Trevor behaves the way he does, and they have no idea what to do about it. However, with a clear understanding of the characteristics of Asperger Syndrome you can see where the trouble spots were, and what ultimately caused the situation to spiral out of control for Trevor's family. In case you missed any of them, here they are.

Difficulty communicating with peers. People with AS often do not understand reciprocity; that is, I take a turn speaking, you take a turn speaking, and so on. Trevor wanted to TELL the kids about his "special interest," Pokémon, like delivering a lecture. This didn't fly well; they weren't interested.

Difficulty playing with his peers. Trevor was afraid to climb on the play equipment. Why? Because he has problems with balance and he's afraid he'll fall. This meant he was left out of the activity all the other kids enjoyed.

Trouble in line. The nature of lines often involves bumping, which is hard for someone with vestibular (balance) and proprioceptal (body awareness) problems. Trevor lost his balance, over-corrected, and crashed into the lady ahead of him.

No luck at potluck. The good thing about potlucks is the surprise factor and being able to try new things. Not for Trevor! He has problems with food because he only can tolerate certain tastes and textures. Casseroles are too unpredictable in taste and texture because of their mixed, often indistinguishable ingredients, and salads taste bitter to him.

Failed reward. Offering a reward at the right time can be an incentive to stick it out through an uncomfortable situation. Trevor's dad had the right idea by mentioning dessert, but things went awry because that wasn't something that he could necessarily deliver. Also, Trevor wasn't able to clearly communicate his thoughts about having a piece of his favorite kind of pie. This is partly due to the "theory of mind" deficit many people with AS experience. That is, he couldn't predict the actions of others. He had decided that was his pie; therefore it was. He was unable to predict that someone else might take it.

When you lay it out point by point based on the right information, Trevor's behavior makes perfect sense. It is obvious to us what went wrong for him. His parents are trying so hard, but they feel they are failing miserably. Then on top of their son's bewildering behavior, they are faced with the judgment of others: The mother who says, "Let them work it out." The woman in line who scowls at them when their son falls into her. The well-intentioned pie lady who offers to make him a pie "next time," which meant absolutely nothing to Trevor who was in the middle of a meltdown (plus when is "next time?"). And finally, the parents' overall sense that they are being watched, measured and falling short of the parenting mark by all the people at the park, or at the very least, *their perception that they are.*

It's no wonder they don't want to go back to another community potluck! They are disappointed and feel cheated out of happy moments that other parents take for granted. And together they worry about Trevor, their ability to effectively parent him and what will happen in the future. They wish they knew what to do.

So, what do Trevor's parents do? And what do WE do when faced with these kinds of situations? Look no further than this book to find out. Here's a sneak preview of what you'll find.

Overview of the Book

Chapter 1: Who Are You? Tools for Navigating the Inner World of the Asperger Parent. This is where we reflect on where we are, and how we feel about being an Asperger Parent. Think of it as your first line of defense against the misjudgment of others, and against self-criticism.

Chapter 2: Don't Leave Home Without It! The Asperger Parent Survival Kit: Tools for Effective Parenting. This chapter lays out the basics, tools you can apply to a variety of situations and settings.

Chapter 3: One Pie, Too Many Slices! Tools for Balancing Everyone's Needs. Not enough of you to go around? Learn why taking care of yourself is the first step in finding family balance.

Chapter 4: Reaching Out: Tools for Building a Community of Support. We'll always face judgment, but with the right support, you feel accepted, and it doesn't sting as much because you have reinforcements who back you up. In addition to pointing out how to capitalize on these supports, the chapter gives you a few tips for dealing with the people who are less than helpful.

Chapter 5: A Marriage of Inconvenience: Tools for Building a Relationship with the School. Your child's educational needs can sometimes make for strange bedfellows, metaphorically speaking! Here are a few tips to hopefully move it from merely tolerable to successful, and ideally even amiable.

Chapter 6: Sanctuary: Tools for Creating a Comfortable Home Environment. Home is our sanctuary. This chapter presents practical ideas for making home a more peaceful place for the entire family.

And finally, if you're wondering what happens to Trevor's family, stay tuned and find out!

No Book Police will be sneaking around to ensure you start from the beginning of the book instead of skipping right to the tools and practical ideas you need right NOW. You might discover, however, as many of us have, that tools alone don't do the trick. As parents we need to understand the emotions that are driving us, as they help or hinder how we move through the world with our AS child. An important component of this is addressed in Chapter 1, *Who Are You? Tools for Navigating the Inner World of the Asperger Parent.*

Why is it important to answer this question for yourself in connection with a book about practical solutions for the home? Because until you recognize and reconcile how you see yourself and your family, you cannot fully utilize tools that often run counter to conventional parenting norms. Knowing yourself allows you to implement the tools with an ever-increasing sense of sureness. When you are faced with those moments of challenging behaviors with your child, you will draw from that reserve of knowing. It will give you the strength and confidence to be able to say to yourself, "I am doing the right thing. I am meeting my child's needs."

Chapter 1

Who Are You?

Tools for Navigating the Inner World of the Asperger Parent

Your world changes the day your child receives a diagnosis of Asperger Syndrome. It is the key to understanding so many of the puzzling behaviors you've experienced with him, and it is the jumping ground from which you start the next phase of your family life. But along with this revelation, your secret identity has been revealed: You are "Parent of Child with Autism." The world now views you through this lens; it is *your* label. There are days when you assume this role as a reluctant burden, and at other times you embrace it with pride. Days when you can take on the world with your newfound Parent of Child with Autism superpowers, and days when you want to pull the covers over your head and say, "I quit."

In this chapter we'll discuss the impact diagnosis has on the Asperger Parent, how we are perceived by others and, most important, how we perceive ourselves. So, on the days we feel like quitting, we'll be able to pull out the tools and find the resources to get up and take on the world one more time.

The New Status Quo

Perhaps you didn't realize the dubious perks that come along with your Parent of Child with Autism merit badge. If you haven't yet been informed, here's what's in store for you.

Like it or not, you have just become your community's official spokesperson for Asperger Syndrome. Once people become aware of your new "status," not only do they ask you personal questions about your child, they ask you about autism spectrum disorders in general. And if you are reasonably informed and well spoken, look out! The questions get harder, but don't worry; eventually they become repetitive and you'll be able to answer in your sleep.

You have something everyone wants – your phone number!
After you've been grilled sufficiently by the curious, you'll eventually realize there's an ulterior motive. The more questions, the more likely they'll ask for your phone number because they have a grandson, nephew, or know someone who has a child with autism, and they desperately need to access your resources.

You get free career counseling. Everyone suddenly has ideas about how you spend your time. Enthusiastic folks present you with an endless supply of ideas about what you should be doing with your new-found expertise – start a support group, write a book, speak, be involved in politics. Because everyone knows, you couldn't possibly have enough to do already!

You are now extremely popular! Sometimes expectations come from within the autism and disability community. You may feel obligated to join a multitude of organizations and to be heavily involved in all of their fundraisers and activities. They want and need bright, active parents such as you to help with the growing need within every community.

All this may be flattering, but it may also feel like added pressure. It's important to recognize that you can do these things if you want to. Many parents feel great satisfaction in being involved in all these activities. But it should be because *you* want to, not because you feel pressured. Your priority, first and foremost, is your family's well-being. And your own well-being. You are not obligated to do everything other people think you should! You choose; you decide.

More Labels

Under the title of Parent of Child with Autism you might also carry other labels, particularly if you are actively involved with your child's education and therapy. You are:

"The Perfect Parent": Self-sacrificing, attentive and cooperative. This in itself is a pretty high standard to try to maintain, but when you're The Perfect Parent others praise how well you are handling things ... implying you don't have any needs. AND, these are the very same people who ask you to do more. Or:

"The Parent from Hell": *Overly involved, nit-picky, know-it-all.* You're the squeaky wheel that gets the grease – the parent who has strong opinions, the one who demands services for her child, and often gets them. The double-edged sword is that you may be equally effective and disliked when you are the Parent from Hell.

What is the reality? Are you one or the other? Most actively involved parents are a mixture of both, or somewhere in the middle. Sometimes you are patient and self-sacrificing, sometimes you are a thorn in the side of every school administrator you come into contact with. Parents are human beings with emotions like everyone else, but because of the nature of your "job" as Parent of Child with Autism you have many more occasions to bring out your multiple personalities and put them to work advocating for your child.

My Reputation Precedes Me

While it's important to listen to constructive feedback and perceptions from others, don't always believe your own press. It's too restrictive and confining.

Maintain an identity separate from your Asperger Parent persona. Think of your role as a parent advocate as if you are merely putting on work clothes for the job of getting the services your child needs. It is only part of who you are.

Surround yourself with close friends who care about and see you as YOU. Real friends give you the kick in the pants you need when you're dropping the ball, and they also inform you when you've crossed the line from "passionate" to pain in the neck.

So who ARE you? That's for you to decide. But to do that, first you have to assess where you are now.

Good Grief!

How did you react when your child was first diagnosed? Maybe you cried, or maybe you cut yourself off from friends and family for a while. Or perhaps you did just the opposite: sought out extra support from the people who care about you. That is the kind of behavior we generally expect when someone has received such life-altering news. Everyone expects there will be an initial time of grieving; after all, you're experiencing the loss of the dreams you had for your child.

Upon hearing the diagnosis, you had all these questions: What does this mean for his future? Will he be able to live independently? Hold down a job? Get married and have children? What will happen to my child? For many of us the predominant thought is, What do we do now?

Where Are You?

Everyone deals with the shock of diagnosis differently, some better than others. And then there are those who just *appear* to be handling it better. Check in to see if any of the following reactions appears familiar to you.

Nobody's home. Some parents become stuck and cannot move forward. They are mired in grief. For some this lasts only a short time; others continue to be unable to untangle their emotions enough to move to the next step. And because they never reconcile their feelings, they are trapped in that moment of diagnosis forever. These are often the parents who don't do anything to help their child obtain services or therapy because they are struggling just to deal with daily life. They may shrug sadly because they think, "What's the point?"

Half checked in, half checked out. Parents who fall into this category are in a state of permafrost too, but are able to meet at least *some* of their child's needs. Their child may be receiving some services and interventions from the school; perhaps they even take him to therapy because they've been told this is what they are supposed to do. They might show up, but they aren't plugged in. They allow others to make the decisions about their child because they assume the professionals – the school, the doctor, the state – know what is best for their child.

The Perfect Parent rides again! On the other side of the scale are parents who don't appear to grieve much at all. They take off like someone has lit a fire under them. They may have been actively seeking answers for years and seem almost elated at having a diagnosis. Finally, we know what it is! That initial rush to learn about Asperger Syndrome can toss these parents into a frenzy of conducting research on the Internet, reading and fervent networking.

You may have been, or may be right now, the type of parent who is completely driven with the project of doing everything possible to help your child. Overnight your entire world revolves around your child's disability – sometimes to the exclusion of everything else. If you are one of these kinds of parents, you might hear comments like, "You have such a great attitude!" And indeed, you might be the picture-perfect coping family and your child might be doing well. OR, you might just LOOK like you're doing well.

Blindsided

Things are moving along nicely, or so you thought. Finding yourself hit with any of the situations below can either kick-start a downward spiral or might signal that one has already started.

Unexpected turn for the worse. Maybe you find out your insurance company will not cover occupational therapy, or maybe there's a problem at your child's school. He might be going through a rough period, or maybe there is a serious problem you have to spend a great deal of time not only worrying about, but also trying to fix.

Pressure builds. There will be extra stress on your life. That's a given. Maybe you've spent so much money on evaluations and therapy, and the gas to get there, that financial pressure begins to build.

Your body betrays you. Maybe you don't sleep well, or you're eating too much. Maybe you feel cranky all the time; you snap at your family. You might cry without warning, or you never cry about anything. You might be having migraines, stomach ailments or getting sick with every bug that comes along. You become so accustomed to this state that you don't realize it's out of the ordinary, or that there might be a reason behind it.

Realization hits. You might look around and realize that you are missing out on a lot of things you used to do, and it hits you that you aren't living a typical family life. These things build on each other and can eventually send a parent into a tailspin without warning. This might happen six months, a year, or even more, after your child's diagnosis, long after you thought you'd resolved your feelings about it. You think, "What is happening to me?!" And "Why is this happening now?!"

The Question Remains

Parents of neurotypical children do not have a telescope that allows them to look into the future and see their children become functional, independent, successful adults, but they kind of work from that assumption. We have a model of what that looks like: possibly college, career, marriage and children. Whether it is completely realistic or not, that's generally how the thinking goes.

However, when your child is diagnosed with an autism spectrum disorder, that vision of the future is permanently shattered. The future seems murky and fraught with obstacles. You are caught up in your child's current needs, but in the back of your mind is always the niggling worry of what will be. You don't have a mental model to go by because you don't know what skills and abilities your child will have at 18, at 25 or even 30 years old. When your child makes progress in one area, optimism blooms and the future seems filled with endless possibilities for him. But when he isn't doing well, the unknown sends you into despair. An issue such as the insurance company refusing to pay for occupational therapy isn't just about the short term, "But my son is having trouble dressing and grooming himself and he can't tie his shoes!" In your heart you may worry, "If my son can't dress and groom himself, he's going to be like the homeless guy I saw today with matted hair and no shoes!" *The reason grief is shadowing you now is that you still do not know the answer to the question you asked when your child was first diagnosed,* "What will happen to my child?"

Grief Is Mourning the Loss of What Will Never Be

When your child has a neurological disability, from time to time you will be hit by new realizations of what this loss means for your child. It is like a spiral maze made up of rings of grief. There is the initial circle where you receive the news of your child's diagnosis. You adjust and make the turn toward the future, thinking you are done with grieving. Then unexpectedly you encounter another turn, and another ... and another. With each new obstacle or challenge, with each new step of development as you must again face the reality of how his challenges affect your child's life, you may find yourself spiraling once more. For example, "My son is 16; he should be able to get his driver's license." Or, "Now he's 18, and he should be going off to college, but he's not ready; maybe he'll never be able to live on his own." Your grief may come and go like this for the rest of your life. You can't say, "I'm done with it forever," because you continue to have the same questions you had at the beginning of the process, "What will happen to my child?" It is the never-ending question.

While your grief may continue, you will be in a much better position to cope if you give it recognition. Denying how much it hurts won't make it go away; in fact, it'll seep into every aspect of your life. Face the deepest fears of your heart over your child's future, and allow yourself the recognition that your job is hard. You have a right to take the time to acknowledge it hurts and to honor the pain and sorrow you are feeling. Mourning the loss of the dreams you had for your child doesn't mean you will be frozen in grief. It means you are facing your fears and the significance of what has happened to you and your family before moving on to the next step.

This is your reality. You may fear this flood of emotions, especially if you have pent them up for a long time. It may seem as though the tears will never stop, but they will (don't worry, you're just "defrosting!"). And in the meanwhile, know that these tears are the tide that will propel you forward. Sail on.

It's important to make a side note here. If you are crying and withdrawn for more than two weeks at a time, or have other recognizable signs of depression such as insomnia, exhaustion, irritability, loss of interest in formerly pleasurable activities, significant weight loss or gain, excessive feelings of guilt or worthlessness, please seek help! Ignoring it as you press on not only does not serve you well, it doesn't help your child either. You have a long journey ahead of you as a parent of a child with autism, and he needs you to be healthy. See a psychologist or, if you think you need medication, a psychiatrist. You would never stand for your child to suffer that way; it's not okay for you to suffer either.

Recognize the signs. A couple of years ago we began taking our son to our psychologist, Joe, for behavior management consulting. In addition to addressing our son's needs, Joe often turned to me at some point during our visits and asked, "How are YOU doing, Mom?," in a tone that said it wasn't just a polite social question. I invariably bristled – we weren't here to talk about me. "I'm fine. I'm handling things. See, I'm a 'good mom' who always puts her child's needs first!" These were my thoughts, but my reply was simply, "Fine," as I brushed him off with a polite smile that was intended to convey, "None of your business."

This pattern continued until one day Joe said to me, "I think you're depressed." Again, I scoffed, but as I considered his remark, I began to wonder if he might just be right. My friends confirmed these suspicions, "You never talk about gardening any more." "You haven't gone out with us for ages!" I finally swallowed my pride, and confessed, "Okay, Joe, maybe you're right."

He then proceeded to give me a depression scale survey to fill out. In my usual way, I leaned a little more toward the optimistic side of things. After tallying my responses, Joe looked over the paper with raised eyebrows and said, "56." I promptly countered, "Oh, that's not bad; right in the median range. What's normal?" He said, "Five." My mouth dropped open. Five? Ha! Who is *that* happy?

Joe was right! I had burned out over a long period of time, years, in fact, and hadn't realized it. I was too busy running myself ragged to have noticed. I thought if I didn't do everything humanly possible to help my children, if I slacked off for just one minute, I'd destine them to a life of utter misery. That was how I was dealing with my grief. I finally stopped a moment, took stock of things and began to take better care of myself, so I could truly move forward once more. There is an important lesson here: *Not only did I get help for myself, my children benefited as well.*

As it turned out, in taking care of my own needs, I built up a reserve of strength just in time for a major crisis. It wasn't the first crisis in our family, and I know it won't be the last. So this mom is on the maintenance plan, tuned up and ready to go so I can take care of my children for the long term. This isn't a sprint; it's a marathon. I'm pacing myself.

Fine Isn't FINE!

"How are you?" goes the polite social question. "Fine" is usually the corresponding polite answer, but it doesn't necessarily mean, "I'm okay." "Fine" is really a secret code word with multiple meanings such as:

"You wouldn't understand, so why should I bother explaining?"

"And anyway, you don't REALLY want to know!"

"Sigh, this is my life; I try not to think about it."

"I'm answering 'fine' so you'll go away."

"My life sucks, thank you very much for asking!"

"You think there is something wrong with me, don't you?"

"Stop looking at me because I might cry."

"I don't really know HOW I feel so I'm just going to be polite."

"How would YOU feel, buddy? Want to trade places?"

"None of your business."

The Keys to Acceptance

If grief is mourning the loss of what will never be, acceptance means creating a new vision for your child's future. How do you do that? And how do you reconcile your own feelings in order to move forward?

Creating a New Vision

As parents of a child with Asperger Syndrome it often seems as though you are constantly putting out fires. In addition to the challenges most parents face on a regular basis, you have school, therapy and medical issues, among others, to deal with, as well as your child's direct needs. In the midst of meeting these demands, it is hard to think about the future. Some parents purposely shy away from thinking about how the immediate goals affect their child's future because so many variables can enter into the picture. Due to the "Swiss cheese" nature of Asperger Syndrome, your child may have high-level skills in one area and low-level skills in another. He may be academically brilliant, for example, but his social skills might be lacking. There are no clear-cut answers to what his abilities will be as he enters adulthood.

While no parent can see the future in a crystal ball, you can help things move in the right direction when you create a realistic vision and clear goals for your child. Parents need to think long term in small increments. Your child may not "look" like every other child, and when he grows up he may not look like every other adult either. It is important to see your child as the unique person he is, to focus on his strengths, and use those skills and abilities to envision a future you are both excited about. There is a fine line between facing reality and remaining optimistic about your child's future. You will be straddling it constantly, trying to find balance between the two.

Get a Reality Check About Your Child's Future

You won't know exactly what your child's skills will be like at 18, but remember there are many adults with Asperger Syndrome who grew up with no diagnosis, no support, and no therapy and yet are functioning quite well. Now look at your own child. Your child is well taken care of, you are seeking to understand his needs and will guide him into adulthood with not only competence, but with excellent care. You are seeking services on his behalf. The odds are greatly in his favor.

Don't let yourself get overly caught up with milestones. There is so much pressure in our society for children to become independent at increasingly younger ages, but all children develop on their own timeline. Don't let benchmarks and goals become more important than who the child is becoming.

Do not only focus on what is relevant to your child now. Take a look at materials and books that are related to older children and young adults. All children grow up more quickly than we'd like (most days!). Having a roadmap for what you might expect helps you have more confidence in what you're doing right now.

Find out what transition services are available in your community for individuals with disabilities. Although things will change over time, use what you know as a base for understanding what your child might be eligible for as he enters adulthood. Some parents assume they'll be completely left to their own devices, which makes their child's future seem frightening to them. Others have unrealistic expectations of their community's services and, as a result, do not have a safety net to catch their child in adulthood.

Get to know adults in the AS community. They often can give you insight into how your child experiences the world and what you can do to help him. Take a good look and recognize the beauty of who he is, and you'll see your child in a different light.

Encourage your child to dream. When a neurotypical child says, "I want to be a doctor when I grow up!," good teachers and parents do not look askance or discourage him. If your AS son says he's going to be an engineer and work for the Lego Corporation some day, who says he can't? Use that statement to help him focus on his immediate goals and equip him with the skills to achieve that dream step by step. And allow yourself to dream with him. If you're thinking it's impossible for him to achieve his dreams, YOU will be the biggest obstacle he has to overcome.

Embrace Your Child's Uniqueness

It often seems as though we can only focus on what's "wrong" with our kids. We get caught up in the whirlwind of daily struggles and can't see the big picture. We see "autism" instead of seeing our child. We see negative behavior in every aspect of Asperger Syndrome, instead of recognizing the charm of who the child is. We are shortchanging our child when we do this, and we cheat ourselves of pride and pleasure as we watch him grow.

Put on your Asperger-colored glasses. Don't just look at your child's behavior, SEE your child. For example, after what I perceived as a grueling Yu-gi-oh monologue from my son, his therapist, Joe, said, with a twinkle in his eye, "I wish Asperger Parents could step back and see how endearing their kids are." Instead of interpreting every odd behavior as a negative, appreciate your child as having character. Listen to his voice pattern, watch his mannerisms and recognize the beauty of how he speaks. Smile at the use of the big words he uses that he may, or may not, understand, but somehow manages to interject appropriately.

I FIND THAT EXTRAORDINARY!

Experience the delight of their passion. Many people do not feel strongly about anything, much less find tremendous joy and satisfaction in their lives. But our kids often have the gift of knowing exactly what it is that drives them – their special interest. They are passionate about it. It can help them live fulfilling lives that many neurotypicals only dream of. Witnessing this is inspiring and infectious. Revel in it. Then use it to help your child find the direction of his life in a related career.

Tune in to his world. Your child has a take on the world that you've probably never encountered before and could never think up on your own. For example, while everyone else is busy making eye contact during a conversation, he is seeing a world you don't even notice. Some of our kids are told to be quiet so often that they learn to keep their thoughts to themselves, but if you're very lucky, your child might share them with you. Don't be surprised if you don't always understand what he's saying, because, frankly, he might be smarter than you, at least when it comes to his special interest!

Conduct Your Own Reality Check

"It's hardest on the parents." Have you heard this one yet? Statements like this have been uttered by many compassionate professionals to AS parents. It is a common thought that somehow when children are suffering, the parents feel it more than the child. It's important to remember that if we are distressed, imagine how our child must feel! He is the one feeling what is happening to him. Think about *his* perspective.

Our kids may not have a clear understanding about what is happening. For example, you think YOU are bewildered when he has a meltdown, how do you think he feels? He is unable to communicate his needs effectively and has no way to meet them himself at that point. It's like a firestorm in his brain and he has no escape. There are other things he experiences first-hand such as his social and sensory difficulties. Yes, you *worry* about him, which is painful, but he's the one who is actually *feeling* these things.

Time is a difficult concept to grasp. As adults we have the ability to take into consideration our knowledge and experience that difficult times come and go. For example, if we are doing an unpleasant task, we know that it will eventually end. Our children do not have a long-term perspective or sense of time to know when or if something will end.

Focus on Being Grateful

It's easy to get caught up in what we have to grouse about. We struggle on so many fronts as parents of a child with AS: emotionally, financially, socially … the list goes on endlessly. But there is a stark difference between acknowledging your emotions and endlessly wallowing in them. Wallowing drags us down; we flounder in helplessness and stew in bitterness. Instead, hope and optimism are born out of gratitude for the things we DO have. And there is much to be grateful for.

This is the best time to date for a child to have Asperger Syndrome. Until a short time ago, no one understood what AS was or how to help kids like ours. In this era of the Internet and global communication, we can take advantage of exponential expansion of ideas and the ability to access them! Brilliant minds are diligently churning out new theories, ideas and interventions to help our children achieve their highest potential.

Increased public awareness. The media is now focusing on autism spectrum disorders. As the community learns more about families like ours, people are more likely to understand, accept and make adjustments for our children.

Take a look around. We're lucky to be living in a first-world country where we have laws to protect our children and our rights as parents, and where we have access to services. No, it's not perfect. Improvements are badly needed in many areas. But in the meanwhile, let's be thankful for what we do have.

The comparison game. Okay, so generally it's not a good idea to compare yourself to others, but we all do it. We find ourselves being envious of families who are unencumbered by the worries that many AS parents carry. Typically, they don't worry that their child is going to have a meltdown at the grocery store, if insurance is going to cover therapy or if their child will ever be able to live independently. Well, since we compare anyway, take it to the extreme. Your child is alive. And you are here to comfort and help him. When the tsunami in Asia hit, I'll bet more than one parent thought, "Tidal wave or autism? Hm, autism isn't such a bad gig after all." You can always find someone who is suffering more than you are.

Embrace Life

What is the opposite of wallowing in bitterness? It is giving yourself permission to feel pleasure and joy. Sometimes as Asperger Parents we feel obligated to put on a happy face for others, but are we also doing the same thing with our sad face? Are we looking morose because we think we're supposed to feel and act that way as a parent of a child with a neurological disorder?

If you view life as something you have to endure, that's no fun, and it certainly isn't going to have you jumping for joy over having a family like yours. Lighten up!

Live in the moment. It seems like a contradiction to say this while you are always keeping an eye out for potential problems and long-term goals. This is hard to do when you are bombarded with crisis after crisis, and are always waiting for the other shoe to drop. But you can't live your life that way. Don't allow yourself to be robbed of now. Take a cue from our AS kids, who are where they are "right now." When they are sad, they are sad; when they are happy, they are happy.

Recognize your own wisdom. Your experiences as an Asperger Parent have helped you develop a rich inner world and strength of spirit. Use the empathy you've developed from having experienced grief to reach out to someone else and provide support. Maybe it's just offering the comfort of listening and a shoulder to lean on. This has the added benefit of making you feel better.

Find your funny bone! Stop being so serious all the time. Right in the middle of the worst situation, the funniest things often happen. Your child might even say something that is funny during a meltdown. We aren't laughing at that moment, but later behind closed doors giggle about it. Laughing about it isn't making fun of your child. And just think, all those embarrassing public humiliations are fodder for family lore. Step back even when you're in the middle of them and think, "I'm going to laugh about this later. Not now, but boy will it be funny in a couple of hours ... or days, or ... years!"

Twelve Good Things About Having Three Children with Asperger Syndrome

- I finally have an answer when people say, "What about the third one, does she have it too?" And they've stopped asking me, "What causes it?" Instead they just eye me suspiciously.

- If I've made salad, broccoli or asparagus for dinner I can have it all to myself. In fact, I can sit by myself as well.

- Our children are never embarrassed by their siblings' bad behavior in public. If they even notice their brother or sister is flopping around screaming on the floor in a restaurant, they don't find it distressing ... or even unusual.

- Three words: Shared Special Interests. I'm not exactly sure what Neopets are, but rest assured that there is at least one sibling who does – and, more important, knows where to find it on the Internet.

- I have three people who can remind me what The Rules are at all times in case I forget. Such as, it's wrong to drive over 55 miles per hour and I should not litter. If I'm especially lucky, someone will throw in an explanation about global warming too.

- After one trip to the store with the kids, my husband believes me and will pick up anything I want on his way home from work.

- I can hide candy in the vegetable drawer of the refrigerator because no one will EVER look there.

- The school secretary knows my voice even before I tell her my name.

- Because none of my children can stand the sound of their classmates singing in music class, we are not required to attend boring school programs.

- When the small-town newspaper mentions a 300% increase in the number of children with autism in our school district, I take personal pride in the fact that they are specifically talking about my family.

- I never have to wonder if I have bad breath. Someone always tells me.

- And best of all: All those medical deductions on our income tax return mean a big fat refund check – Legoland here we come!

This kind of attitude relieves the tension and eases your frustration. It helps you maintain a perspective of this just being a moment of difficulty that WILL pass. Ask yourself, will I remember it tomorrow as completely heart-breaking, or is there some dark irony in it? And, "It is what it is." This is your reality. You can run from it, or embrace it, but either way it just IS. Not accepting it won't make it go away.

There is no end to this list because you have your own keys to acceptance. Think about how much you know about your child, about Asperger Syndrome and about so many other things. You already have a sense of what you want and need to move forward; give yourself permission to take that step.

Steel

If people say that raising a child with a disability, or a child period, is a picnic every day, frankly, they are fibbing. As Autism Parents we have unique challenges. A good day for us is one that might be in the top ten worst ones for another family. But we grasp it with both hands and embrace it. Who knows? Tomorrow might be worse. We try not to lose sight of how special it is, and how incredible our kids are. A bad day is when we want to go back in time and do things differently. How far back? Depends on how bad the day is. Maybe just far enough to start over and not be so crabby next time. Or it might be as far back as the day my husband and I said to each other, "it's time we started our family." Not because we don't love our children, or don't want them, but because at times we feel so inadequately equipped for the job of raising them. Most days are not that bad, but sometimes ...

Are there days I'd truly like to take back? Of course. But not the ones you might think. Not the days the kids were diagnosed, as painful as those were. Instead, I'd like to take back the moments when I've been impatient, when I barked at the kids and when I complained about how much trouble they were. But I really don't want to take back the days that were hardest for me. The ones when I was pressed from all sides by the insurance company, the school and the kids all at the same time. The times when I was at my lowest, when I felt my weakest, when I was most isolated and hurting. The days I thought would never end. Because those are the days that taught me the most about how to accept my shortcomings and created an inner core of strength I would never have imagined myself capable of. Those are the days when I learned how to be my fiercest and strongest, and also how to become most tender with myself and the people I love. Those are the days I touched other people's hearts by allowing myself to be vulnerable and to accept help – the days that taught me to have compassion for myself and an increased understanding of the suffering of others.

Are there days I'd like to erase for my children? Of course. I'd like to take away every day they've been hurt or cried because of other people's inability to understand their needs, especially when I was the one who didn't understand them. I'd like to remove from their memory banks the heart-breaking moments when they struggled with feeling lost, alone and misunderstood. I'd like for them to have only happy moments that make them smile. But I'd be wrong in protecting them like that. Because those are the very things that tested their strength too and are making them into the insightful, creative and empathetic human beings they are becoming.

I think happiness is overrated. Maybe we aren't supposed to be blissfully happy every moment, or even most of the time. Maybe the best we can hope for is to be close, to share the painful times in our lives and to find forgiveness for each other and for ourselves. It is what makes us human after all, the ability to recognize in ourselves and others what is weakness, what is sorrow, and how to find tenderness and bridge the gap between us with grace.

Nara steel is the strongest in the world. It is forged by beating the metal thin and bending it over again and again – as many as 10,000 times. This is what creates its strength. Do I wish to be continually pounded until I am so thin I can't do anything but bend? Absolutely not. But it isn't my choice. Despite myself, I will be steel. And so will my children.

Embarrassment

Are you embarrassed by your child's behavior? When he was throwing himself on the floor of the grocery store at age two, you got some annoyed looks. Others looked on with recognition because their kids had done the same thing. Some may have said in an almost cheerful tone, "Terrible twos!" And you were somewhat comforted, hoping this meant that when he turned three it would stop. But it didn't. As he grew, four, five, six, and it continued, there were no longer sympathetic looks; instead there was judgment (especially when he is 12! Trust me on this.). You feel as though you can read their minds, "Spoiled brat." "Bad parent."

Finding the correct diagnosis is often a salve to parents' hearts in that they now know why their child falls apart at the grocery store. And as parents we can develop tools to prevent some of these public meltdowns, but they still might happen. Even when we attempt to predict everything that can go wrong and plan for every contingency, our child will still have difficult days and sometimes will embarrass us.

This is stressful for parents for a number of reasons. First, we feel bad that our child is in distress. Second, we have to abandon what we are doing to deal with behavior issues – sometimes a whole trip is a total bust.

But often we are most bothered by our own embarrassment over the child's behavior. Why? Because instead of seeing him through the eyes of a compassionate parent, we are seeing him through the world's eyes. We judge him as the world judges him, and we judge ourselves right alongside.

No matter how well you prepare and how hard your child tries, he won't always be able to hold it together. As hard as it is for us to deal with the challenges of having a child with a neurological disability, imagine how he feels. The environment around him is not well suited to meet his needs, yet he must traverse it daily. He must constantly abandon his comfort zone and go out into a harsh and foreign land that he doesn't completely understand, and whose inhabitants do not understand him. If he is aware of these obstacles to his well-being, imagine how it feels.

Mercifully, some of our kids have little or no awareness of the harsh judgments of others, but can they be immune to judgment from their own parents? Probably not. Even if we don't verbally express it, our unease and tension are painfully obvious even to them at times. Also, despite our best intentions, we might let it affect our behavior and parenting at that moment by being impatient or inflexible. Therefore, it is crucial that we, above all people, develop the ability to discern when our child is doing the best he can, and then take responsibility for helping him negotiate his way through the world. We must not allow other people's, albeit possibly well-intentioned, criticism of our child's behavior or their misperception about our parenting skills to negatively impact our interactions with him.

What can we do to combat our embarrassment and ensure we continue to meet our child's needs? A major remedy is to hold realistic expectations for your child.

Understand the characteristics of Asperger Syndrome and how they affect his life. He isn't going to behave the way other children do. You will continue to face challenges.

Observe your child and take note of what tends to set him off in public situations. Increase the odds of future successful experiences by using tools such as priming and predicting, rewards and wrap-up – more about that in Chapter 2.

Build a support system that reinforces your values and views about how children and adults with autism should be treated. This will thicken your skin to criticism because you have back-up for your strong inner voice that says "I know what I'm doing; I am meeting my child's needs."

Have a sense of humor. I cannot stress this enough! Our kids do and say some of the funniest things because their perspective is unique. Appreciate it! It's reasonable for us to be sorry if our child has done something that is hurtful or harmful, but short of that, if we have a sense of humor about it, so will most other people, especially if you clue them in. And if they don't, remember: Some of the most horrifically embarrassing public situations make the best family stories.

Community Outreach and Education

I'll share my secret with you. I used to care way too much about what people thought. True, I have a giant chicken painted on my garage, but that's "eccentric," which is perfectly acceptable in a small town. It gives folks something to gossip about at the gas station. But embarrassment was the worst horror imaginable to me. Parenthood helped me get a grip – the baby barfs (or worse!) on you when you're out and you've brought a change of clothes for the baby, but not for yourself. Or while waiting in line at the grocery store your child informs your fellow shoppers that Daddy says the president is an idiot.

Incidents such as these happen to most parents. But when you have a child with Asperger Syndrome you have *specialized embarrassment.* The same radar that alerts a sleeping baby to wake up when you and your husband are getting romantic is apparently highly attuned in Asperger kids. It seems as if they instinctually know when to embarrass their parents with pinpoint accuracy.

For example, my children have the ability to scream at the precise moment I'm speaking on the phone with my one and only friend who doesn't have kids (much less kids like mine!). This person now has the pleasure of hearing my muffled holler (as I try to cover the receiver with my hand) and frantic hushing of my child, who's informing me that he has been "accidentally poisoned" (his words), as he points to the kitchen table where he has just spat out his lunch because he "felt" there "might" have been a sliver of lettuce in it. (Turns out he was right! A microscopic dot of lettuce had made it from the cutting board to his sandwich.) At least this was a case of "private" embarrassment; it pales in comparison to the public version.

Recently we had another occasion for what I call "Community Outreach and Education," also known as "Taking My Child Out." This was not your run-of-the-mill dose of public humiliation; it involved the double bonus of professional and private citizens as witnesses. We had taken our nine-year-old son in for an MRI at the local hospital. I thought we'd explained the situation clearly to the staff ahead of time and set up sedation upon arrival and anesthesia for the procedure. Yet, after a quick check-in we were directed to ... the waiting room. As we carried our now "reluctant" child into the room, we felt all eyes turn toward us. The kid went off like a rocket. Not only was he scared, he was starved, as the medication he takes makes him ravenously hungry and he hadn't been allowed breakfast before the procedure. So the crowd was entertained by a rousing early-morning wake-up call of "Hungry! Hungry! Hungry!" while our son continued to roll back and forth on the floor crying. This went on for about 10 or 15 minutes until he became overheated, and the tune turned into "Hot! Hot! Hot!" I tried to look as nonchalant as one can while trying to contain a screaming child rolling around at one's feet – all the while attempting not to make eye contact with the witnesses.

I would prefer my children not to be in distress, and I'm not fond of public wrestling sessions with them. But, sometimes it's unavoidable. Being embarrassed is a choice, and I no longer choose to be. Or rather, I try not to be! But embarrassed or not, I will not bow my head in shame. Nor am I usually overly apologetic. (An exception would be the time when my child tried to bite the blood pressure cuff and almost got the medical assistant's fingers. Now that merited an apology.) If I apologized for every inconvenience my children cause, I wouldn't have time for anything else. Our children are doing the best they can, and so are we. My priority at those moments is keeping my child safe. On the other hand, if there is also an opportunity for me to intentionally be overheard saying to my husband, "Poor baby! It's not his fault he has autism," I'll take it! The way I look at it, I'm providing a public service by raising awareness.

Most people are well intentioned. The truth is, they don't know what to say when they encounter the often bewildering behavior of somebody with an autism spectrum disorder. Autism is a puzzle even for the most educated and experienced in the field; no wonder it puzzles the people on the outside looking in. Even if you have evil thoughts of revenge when someone speaks flippantly about what can be incredibly painful for you, try to keep in mind that they just don't understand.

Annoying Things Well-Intentioned People Say

- *"God must have chosen you to have this child."* Okay, on a good day I might even say that myself. On a bad day I might be tempted to strangle someone for making this comment (in my head, that is. I've never actually leapt to anyone's throat – yet). What I really want to say in return is, *"Yes, and God chose you to babysit my son for a week so I can go to Hawaii,"* or simply, *"Well, I don't know what God was thinking that day."*

- *"You're so patient."* One friend counters with, *"I'm not patient, I just have self-control."* My personal take is that when people say, *"You're so patient,"* what they really mean is: *"I could never handle THAT kid. Glad it's you and not me!"*

- *"It's not that bad. Look at him, you can't even tell!"* Translation: I don't believe you – you are making this up. Such a comment could hurt you or make you sputter In outrage, but instead this would be a perfect opportunity to invite the person to take your child to the grocery store, or to sit for a couple of hours listening to him discuss his special interest.

- *"What causes it?"* That is the $64,000 question. Don't we all wish we knew for sure? There are clues, there is research – and there are plenty of people who say they know – but the truth is, we don't know. So why do people ask? I think they are hoping you can tell them so it won't happen to them. If you could say something that merited blame like, *"Oh, I took drugs when I was pregnant,"* they can feel reassured because they didn't and believe that autism therefore will never touch their lives.

The best way to educate people is to avoid reacting to their misspoken words with anything but compassion for their lack of awareness. At least they are asking. Wait and listen, allow yourself to be open to their curiosity. People are hesitant at times to ask the real questions, so they say something upbeat and cheerful, hoping that it really isn't that bad. There are often *real* questions lurking beneath. Show them you are open; try not to take their initial questions and comments too much to heart. Those are the people who are TRYING to understand – know-it-all busybodies on the other hand ... think karma.

Guilt

Guilt is the fuel of parenthood. I wonder if past generations were filled with such guilt, or if our ancestors were too busy "bringing in the sheaves" to think about their potential failures as parents. In any case, guilt is a parent's daily bread these days, and even more so for the parent of a child with autism. Our child's disorder puts more expectations on our plate, it also seems to highlight our inadequacies. I bet the following will sound familiar.

I'm not doing enough! Everyone seems to have an opinion on what you should be doing to treat your child. "If you'd only do this" (fill in the name of any treatment you've ever heard of and even some you haven't but eventually will). Some may even say the word "cure." It can be overwhelming, and some parents become so desperate on their child's behalf that they put all their eggs – time, money, resources – into one basket, only to be told later that it's this other thing that will "cure" their child's autism. Do I need to mention the pangs of guilt that can evoke?

But, maybe it could be better. Even if something is working, you may still harbor the thought that maybe so-and-so is right. If I'd only do such and such, my child would be all right. No matter what course of treatment you choose, you have a nagging doubt at the back of your mind about whether you are doing the right thing. We live in a culture that says everything can be fixed, why not this? Another item to add to the baggage of uneasy guilt you carry around with you.

Everyone wants a piece of me. Other family members want and need pieces of your time that are often taken up by dealing with your child with ASD. As a result, you may feel torn between the child who faces enormous challenges and the child who is doing well but still needs active, involved parents. Most parents find it hard to balance time and attention equally between two or more children. How can you possibly do that when your two children's needs are so vastly different? You can't. Do the best you can, but realize that you'll often feel you are shortchanging somebody. You might as well say, "Yes, I'd like an extra large order of guilt, and yes, I'll have a side of guilt with that and please SUPERSIZE it."

The reality is that you won't be able to do everything, much less do it perfectly. Others will have expectations of you: your family, your friends, the school, the professionals in your lives. You might be beating yourself up with guilt because you feel you are falling so short of the mark. But who set the bar in the first place? Often we take on the expectations of others to the extreme. Maybe it's time we release the expectations of others to focus on what our family needs and on doing the best we can.

When you are mired in guilt, it weighs you down and steals your ability to live in the moment and truly see how much you ARE doing instead of what you are NOT doing. If you continue to focus on the fact that you are not able to do everything, sooner or later you won't have the energy to do anything.

The Guilt That Lurks Beneath

You're continually asked what caused your child's autism, and there is no satisfactory answer. Not for other people, but also not for you. Despite all information to the contrary, you might be having an irrational thought, "It's my fault."

Let's visit that secret worry for a moment. First off, no one knows what causes it. NO ONE. It's easy to look at our family and say, "Well, of course, genetics." In our case we suspect a genetic link, but it doesn't clearly explain why none of either of my husband's or my siblings or their children have Asperger Syndrome, but *all three* of our kids do. And it certainly doesn't explain my friend's children who have the same disorder. It's a mystery. We don't know what causes autism and it's an important question that needs answering. However, our kids are here NOW, and the immediate priority is meeting their needs on a daily basis. Support the research, but don't exhaust your energy mulling over every possible imagined mistake *you* made that caused your child's autism. Guilt is neither merited nor useful in this case.

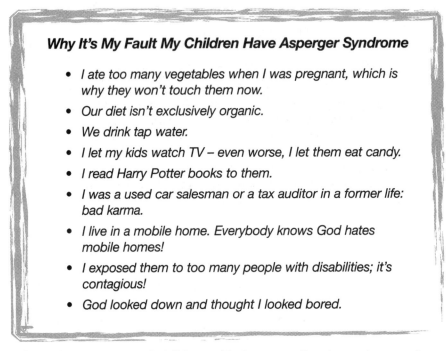

Why It's My Fault My Children Have Asperger Syndrome

- *I ate too many vegetables when I was pregnant, which is why they won't touch them now.*
- *Our diet isn't exclusively organic.*
- *We drink tap water.*
- *I let my kids watch TV – even worse, I let them eat candy.*
- *I read Harry Potter books to them.*
- *I was a used car salesman or a tax auditor in a former life: bad karma.*
- *I live in a mobile home. Everybody knows God hates mobile homes!*
- *I exposed them to too many people with disabilities; it's contagious!*
- *God looked down and thought I looked bored.*

Our role as parents of children with Asperger Syndrome is complex and multi-faceted. We struggle every day with challenges and a kaleidoscope of emotions. Our lives are often so chaotic that it feels as though we are reluctant passengers hanging on to the back bumper of a car going down a twisty road without knowing where we are headed.

But we don't have to be powerless; we can get in the driver's seat. It's true we still won't know what's around the corner, maybe a big ole pothole (my guess is many!). You can't take a detour and get off this road and you can't fill in *every* pothole, although you'll certainly try. But understanding your emotions and dealing with them puts you in the driver's seat and gives you the tools you need for every-thing – from taking care of yourself to parenting your AS child effec-tively. It gives you an arsenal of tools to make adjustments when things go wrong, so when you hit the next big dip in the road you won't spiral out of control. It's up to us alone, because last time I checked, AAA doesn't cover this kind of road service! 🔨

What About Anger?

I purposely didn't give anger a major headline in talking about our feelings. Why? Because too often AS parents are accused of being angry and I don't think it is always an accurate assessment. Sometimes what we really are is frustrated, overwhelmed and just plain exhausted. We're tired of constantly having to fight for services, for having to explain ourselves – and of all the things that go wrong. We look angry, but what is the true underlying emotion? Often I think it's helplessness. We are at the end of our rope and we do not know what to do.

Chapter 2

Don't Leave Home Without It!

The Asperger Parent Survival Kit: Tools for Effective Parenting

The most important tool for effectively parenting a child with Asperger Syndrome is a loving, plugged-in parent. In other words, YOU! If you have a child with Asperger Syndrome, through a combination of loving dedication plus trial and error, you have already developed specialized skills and strategies to help him. You probably don't even realize the multitude of clever adaptations you make every day on his behalf. You know your child better than anyone, and because you love him, you have the most vested interest in helping him become a healthy functional adult. Love is a powerful motivator. And yet, like many parents, you might find that you struggle at times. It's not for lack of love, it's because you haven't been given all the tools you need.

One of the best things about these tools, besides the fact that they just plain WORK, is that once you've learned them, you can take them with you anywhere – no batteries required! Why? Because they are skills, not gadgets. Like all things that are of value, it takes time and effort to learn and implement new skills and strategies for parenting our children. But, what is more valuable than your family? It's worth the initial adjustment for the long-term gain. If it ain't broke, don't fix it. But if things aren't going smoothly the way you're doing things now, it requires trying something new. It's like the saying: If you do it the way you've always done it, then you'll always HAVE what you always HAD.

This chapter presents the basic tools that have been found highly effective for children with autism spectrum disorders. Our kids respond well to structure; it provides the ever-important predictability factor. The nature of these tools is such that they can be used across a variety of situations and settings. Once you understand the concepts, when you are faced with a new situation you won't have to reinvent the wheel every time because it will become second nature. Consider it your Asperger Parenting survival kit. It includes: priming, predicting, countdown, wrap-up and rewards. Included are also strategies for understanding and dealing with meltdowns.

Priming

Priming is used to indicate "What we expect will happen." The child is given clear instructions of what will happen, how it will happen and when it will be over. A sequence of events is outlined, using verbal and sometimes visual directions.

How Do We Prime?

1. *Explanation*. Tell the child what the schedule of events is.

2. *Visual Aids*. Use picture schedules, cartooning or a written list.

3. *Schedule*. Use a timeline and stick to it.

4. *Reward*. Tell, or negotiate, about the reward the child will receive at the end for reasonable compliance, or "going with the program," as best he can.

Predicting

Predicting is speculating on "What might happen." It helps prepare your child for the unexpected, planning for the glitches in the schedule and making alternate plans. This helps the child to understand the possible need for flexibility, and it helps you both foresee potential problems.

How Do We Use Predicting?

1. *Think ahead*. What are the variables that might happen? Use past experiences of what typically sets your child off.

2. *Brainstorm.* Include your child in the process of thinking of what he or you will do if a situation or set of circumstances changes. Keep in mind that both you and your child are much more able to think of "what if" scenarios when calm than when dealing with the aftermath that ensues when you're caught off guard.

Countdown

A countdown is the preparation for an event beginning or ending. It allows the child time to transition from one activity to another.

How Do We Use Countdown?

1. *Remember: The time used in a countdown varies.* Leaving a location, for example, often requires a longer period of adjustment than moving from one activity to another.

2. *Be prepared.* Regardless of whether he can tell time, your child will have a sense of the transition.

3. *Do not count down in seconds (10, 9, 8, 7 ...).* This is too quick of an adjustment for many AS children, and may cause them to panic and have a meltdown.

Wrap-Up

The wrap-up involves assessing the situation afterwards. What worked, what didn't? This can be done with or without your child's input. Analyzing what just happened gives you important information while it is still fresh in your mind about the sequence of events and how you could improve the way things were handled. If you had a positive outcome, you can glean ideas for future successes.

How Do You Use Wrap-Up?

1. *"Just the facts, ma'am."* Keep your voice neutral and do not criticize or scold during wrap-up. Otherwise, your child will be reluctant to discuss what happened, which is counterproductive. It is a time of just listing, play by play, what occurred without judgment.

2. *Wrap-up with your child when he is in a calm state.* If a melt-

down happened, he should be well past the recovery stage before you attempt wrap-up. He may or may not be able to give you insight about what set him off and perhaps even what might help him next time. Your child might not have clear memories of what occurred. However, going over things afterwards to help your child put the pieces together may increase his sense of having some control.

TIPS for Outings

Afraid to go out for fear of what will happen? Too many negative experiences keeping you from braving the cruel world with your child? Don't give up! Here are a few tips to make it go more smoothly next time.

1. **Keep outings short.** *The easier the situation is for your child to endure, the more likely he is to be successful.*

2. **Do what you say you will do.** *Don't say, "We're going to make ONE stop" to entice your child into the car for the outing and then make three. No fibbing, or your child won't believe you next time! Also, don't add more transitions, even fun activities. Things may seem to be going well, but our kids can reach their stress overload threshold quickly.*

3. **Decide on the optimal number of stops.** *Many AS families have rules about only making one or two stops when they go out. Making three transitions in a short period of time is on the outside limit for most AS kids.*

4. **Do the most important thing first.** *If your child is beginning to fray, make sure the last item on the agenda is expendable. This is not necessarily convenient, but compared to the risk of a full-blown public meltdown, it's quite an attractive option.*

5. **Adjust the frequency of outings.** *Some AS families have made the rule that they do not go out as a family two days in a row. Consider a similar arrangement if your child continues to be stressed even when using the tools discussed here.*

Asperger Family Scene

Before Tools

"C'mon son, we're going to the video store to pick out a movie!"

"Hooray! I'm going to get *Pokémon*!!" Parent and child hop into the car and they drive to ... the grocery store. Noticing this change of direction, the child begins to worry if they are going to the video store, and says, "I thought we were going to the video store." In the grocery store, the parent rushes around trying to quickly get what she needs. The child begins to pester his mother and whine, becoming uncooperative. She is hurrying the best she can, but the check-out line is long. Soon the child is lying on the floor, crying. In her frustration, the parent says, "If you don't get up off the floor, we are not going to the video store!"

This threat may or may not help. The child may feel increased anxiety – he's struggling to pull himself together but he's not sure he can. He might already be too overwhelmed to calm himself even with offers of rewards. He may feel further agitated now that he knows there is a good chance he might lose his chance to pick out his video. For her part, the parent is embarrassed by the child's behavior, she's frustrated that the outing is not turning out as she had planned and she can't understand why.

By the time they manage to get through the line (with all the people in the store glaring at them unsympathetically), the child seems to have calmed down and although Mom feels like she's spoiling him after his bad behavior, she drives him to the video store anyway.

Once at the store, her son runs straight for the children's section, where he proceeds to collapse in an enormous meltdown. "They don't have *Pokémon*! They don't have *Pokémon*!" Mom tries to talk him out of it by making several other suggestions, but her attempts are all met with yells of "No, no, no!" through loud sobbing. She finally gives up, picks the unwilling boy up and carries him out kicking and screaming. As he continues to rage in the backseat of the car, her emotions are running high, too. She thinks, "I am a terrible mother and maybe people are right, maybe he IS a spoiled brat."

Preparing for the Same Scenario Using Tools

Now let's look at how tools could be implemented to make things go more smoothly. At the same time it's important to focus on our mind-set in order to give ourselves permission to use them. Dr. Ross Greene (*The Explosive Child*, 2001) says, "Instead of asking yourself, 'What's it going to take to motivate this kid to behave differently?' ask 'Why is this so hard for this child? What's getting in his way? How can I help?'"

Priming
Parent: "We're going to the store; it should take about 20 minutes." Showing the child the grocery list, "I only have to buy milk and eggs so I can make pancakes in the morning. If you're patient, we can stop at the video store afterwards. You can choose ONE movie. You will wait for ME to choose one movie, too. We'll check out. Then we will come home again."

Use of Visuals
People with AS often respond best when given a visual cue, as it is more easily processed than verbal instructions. It's clear, it's concise and, for whatever reason, all of us tend to stick better to something that is down on paper instead of just floating around in our thoughts.

A picture schedule for the current scenario might consist of the following: car, grocery store with milk and eggs, video store, child holding up ONE video, child waiting while parent picks out video, check-out counter. Car. This can be a quick line drawing; you don't have to be an artist.

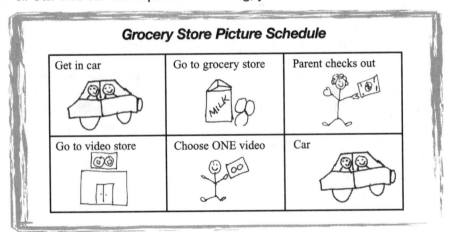

Grocery Store Picture Schedule

Get in car	Go to grocery store	Parent checks out
Go to video store	Choose ONE video	Car

A written grocery list might be sufficient for a child who does not require pictures. Even if a child cannot read, if he can count, he can see how many items must be purchased before leaving the store. Let your child check off or cross out the items if he would like to. It's a nice distraction and feels so grown up.

Predicting

1. *Make the schedule clear.*

   Parent: "We are going to the grocery store first" (use picture schedules if appropriate).

   Parent: "The line might be long at the grocery store. We might need to be patient."

2. *Ask the child questions to check for comprehension and help him problem solve.*

   Parent: "What if the line is long at the grocery store?"

   Child: "I don't want to wait!"

   Parent: "We must wait patiently at the grocery store. No melt-downs. Then we can go to the video store to get a movie. Can you do it?"

   Child considers: "Yes, I guess I can wait so I can go to the video store."

   Next,

   Parent: "What if they don't have *Pokémon*?"

   Child: "They will!"

   Parent: "They might not have *Pokémon*. Let's think of some other movies you might like instead."

3. *Together with the child, think of other possibilities.*

Final Note: If the child says, "No! I can't wait! I don't want any other video besides *Pokémon*," it is time to consider whether you want to risk a meltdown and go anyway, or whether it might be a good night to stay home and see what's on the tube instead.

Reenactment of Scenario Using Tools

Parent and child drive to the grocery store. The child is expecting this stop, so he's not surprised, but since he doesn't like the grocery store, he may start to whine a little. Pointing to the cart, the parent reminds him, "I only have to get eggs and milk, remember?" Seeing she already has eggs, the child knows they are only buying one more item. Mom engages his help in finding the item or lets him push the cart.

When they get to the check-out line, it is long. The child starts to get impatient, but before he gets too agitated, the parent talks with him, "Remember, we talked about this. We knew the line might be long. But we're almost done; you're doing a good job, and in just a few more minutes we'll go to the video store." The child isn't happy, but he pulls it together because he wants to get a video. Parent and child walk out of the store, and he is very excited as they drive to the video store.

When they arrive, he runs straight to the children's section and starts getting upset, "They don't have *Pokémon*!" Close at hand, the parent soothes him, "Remember, we talked about this. We knew it might happen. What other choices did we come up with?" The child thinks and says, "I guess I can get *Scooby-Doo* instead." They check out the *Scooby-Doo* video. In the car on the way home they chat, or at least the mother speaks. She reminds him of the things he did well. She says, "You had a little trouble for a minute at the grocery store, but then you saw we already had the eggs and that we were almost done. I'm proud of you for being patient!" Etc.

This was a successful outing. The child is happy he gets to watch a video – even an alternate title. The parent is happy because even though there were a few small glitches, she feels competent and skilled at helping her child succeed. The next time they go out, they may have even more success. The child may need less prompting because he has learned what to expect. The parent may have gained more confidence because she knows what she is doing works. Notice that the parent kept expectations low to allow the child to experience a successful outing. This is good for the child and for the parent. Remember, positive experiences build on each other and create trust of situations and people.

Rewards

Parents and professionals alike have varying opinions on the issue of rewards. Many adults say that children should conform to rules and social expectations without question, and certainly without compensation. However, this is often not a realistic expectation, particularly for kids with AS.

Think about what you do on your job every day. Is it always easy? How about fun? Are you giddy with anticipation to get to work every single day? Even if you have the best job in the world, not every moment is bliss. So why do you do it? Why do you work so hard?

People work for a variety of reasons, the most obvious being money. You work so you can pay for your living expenses, to buy the things your family needs, and to have money for things you enjoy. Some people are driven by other motivators, such as recognition and prestige.

What about the tasks you perform at home? Do you love doing laundry? Probably not. Yet, you continue to do it, and no one is even paying you. So why do you do it? Perhaps you feel a sense of pride in your family's appearance, or take satisfaction from being able to take care of your family's needs. Your motivation may be as simple as not wanting to smell stinky and look unkempt.

We all have different reasons for why we are willing to perform unpleasant tasks, most of which carry the expectation of being rewarded for hard work whether it is intrinsic (internally motivated) or extrinsic (externally motivated). Why should it be any different for our kids?

Why and How Do Rewards Work?

The trick is finding the right key – rewards – to unlocking cooperation. But why do rewards work so well for kids with Asperger Syndrome?

1. *They respond to extrinsic motivation.* Many of our children do not have the intrinsic motivation to please adults; in fact, they often have to do a great deal of over-riding of their internal resistance to comply with others' expectations. In addition, they also often do not care about recognition or prestige (intrinsic motivation). Therefore, we must find what does motivate them.

2. *They respond to positive reinforcement, particularly when using their special interest.* That is the beauty of setting up a reward system at home; you can create the perfect fit. You may not have to look any further than your child's special interest to find the perfect reward. Does your child long for collectable cards more than anything in the world? Then you've struck gold, because you have the key to cooperation.

Benefits of Using Rewards

1. *It creates a more self-motivated atmosphere. The child wants to perform the task in order to receive his reward.*

2   *It creates a cooperative environment. There is less tension when you are not in a power struggle with your child.*

3. *It teaches your child valuable lessons that may help him realize the benefits of other types of compensation. Your child may realize that he actually enjoys some of the activities you must initially entice him to participate in and chooses to do them on his own in the future.*

4. *It creates a habit that often leads to increasingly greater cooperation. There is ample scientific evidence to show that positive thoughts, experiences and actions, and negative ones, create new neuropathways. With each event, the impulse travels more quickly. Simply put, it burns a path of less resistance. The more you perform a task, the more likely you are to do it again.*

Revisiting the Outing Scenario

The rewards for the outing to the grocery store are already built in, as illustrated below.

Parent: "If you're patient and have no meltdowns, then we can go to the video store" – the cost is waiting; the reward is the video.

The parent may also have a second predictable reward. After the child has chosen his video, he must wait for Mom to pick out hers. In that case, she might tell him, "Be patient and I'll also buy popcorn." Or maybe he knows that whenever they go to the video store and he's well behaved, they always stop at a drive-thru for ice cream.

Other "tricks" include:

- Pack goodies or activities to do in the car or while standing in the grocery line. (Some kids are only allowed to have handheld games under those circumstances, which makes them very appealing.)
- Offer a special snack or treat. Be clear about when the child will receive it. "AFTER we check out, THEN we will go to the car and I will give it to you."
- Allow a trip to the vending machines. Many stores have soda, candy or vending machines with small toys, as well as riding toys. A quarter can buy a great deal of cooperation under the right circumstances.

Using Rewards in Cooperation with the School

Many schools have found that rewards work well for children, so it is one of the most easily accepted adaptations the staff are willing to make for children with AS, especially if the parent will participate or even provide the reward. Remember, they don't want your child melting down on their watch either!

Home-School Connection

Ian was being especially uncooperative at school if he didn't like the subject. During math he often kicked his desk. At other times he would say, "No! I don't want to do it. It's boring!" The teacher sent notes home to his parents day after day describing his behavior. And, just as predictably, Ian's parents talked with him about his attitude and the importance of completing his math, but the situation didn't improve.

They tried to delve deeper, "Is it because you don't like your teacher?" Ian said no. "Is it because it's too hard?" "No," again, followed by "I just don't like it!" Ian's parents were concerned that their son would develop an increasingly negative attitude about math if they didn't find a solution soon. They also worried about how the other kids perceived his behavior and that it would affect him socially. Probing further, they asked "Don't you care what your friends think?" "No," claimed Ian truthfully. Another parent suggested they try taking away something important to him as a punishment. So Ian's parents began to take away his Gameboy if he didn't comply, but that didn't help either. He'd merely stomp off to his room yelling, "It's not fair!" And, disappointingly, his behavior during math didn't improve either.

What do Ian's parents know about him that can help?

- They know he likes Yu-gi-oh cards because they are his special interest.
- They know he likes to play Gameboy.
- They know he likes to eat candy.

These are the things that will motivate Ian.

Ian's parents approached the teacher and worked out a plan to compensate him for good behavior and completing his work at school. The teacher was relieved that they were willing to work as a team with her because Ian was being disruptive to the class. Next, they sat Ian down and explained the system to him.

With a system in place, every day the teacher sends a note home with Ian saying if he did *good*, *great* or *other*, for each class period. The rating is based on (a) having a good attitude and (b) completing his work. For every class where Ian gets a "good" or "great," he receives one penny. If he does something else remarkable that he deserves recognition for, he receives an additional penny. At the end of each day after dinner Ian may use his pennies to "buy" Yu-gi-oh cards or candy from his parents (known motivators). It costs ten pennies to buy one Yu-gi-oh card and five pennies to buy one small piece of candy.

The notes from Ian's teacher almost immediately reflected his efforts to improve his behavior in order to receive pennies. While he didn't complete his work or have a good attitude ALL the time, his behavior improved overall. The system worked so well that his parents continued to use it at home for completing household chores such as feeding the dog, and for achieving behavior goals, such as coming to dinner the first time he was called.

What Does This Teach Ian Beyond the More Immediate Rewards?

- *He learns to work hard to earn something he wants.*

- *He learns that he can do something he doesn't like.*

- *He will learn math, even if he doesn't enjoy it (at the very least, he has to keep track of his pennies!).*

- *He will have a better relationship with his peers and his teacher because his behavior in class is no longer as disruptive.*

- *He and his parents' relationship will improve because there is less conflict between them.*

- *He will associate school with a positive reinforcement (reward) instead of punishment, so ultimately he may like school better. Or, at least feel less aversive to going.*

- *He will be happy with his growing Yu-gi-oh card collection!*

What Happened? It's Not Working Anymore!

After a period of time a reward system may lose its effectiveness. When this happens, you might be tempted to throw up your hands in frustration, but instead it's important to take note of what has changed.

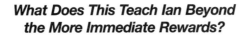

Are you being consistent? Rewards must be given consistently in order for the child to continue to respond to them. He must know with absolute certainty that a given behavior will achieve an expected result.

Has the child lost interest in the reward? Time to pull another rabbit out of your hat! Luckily you know the trick. It might be time for a fresh new reward, or a new system. In the above case, Ian also likes video-games, but his parents have wisely restricted the amount of time he is allowed to play them. This puts it in high demand and is an excellent choice to offer as the next reward. Example: Ian must have a "good" or "great" day overall to earn 30 minutes of videogame time.

Have you tried a reward that is Simply Irresistible? Your child may be able to tolerate the almost unendurable (in his mind) for a bigger reward that he has been dreaming of. For example, he might need to meet a certain expectation of behavior, such as completing his work in three subject areas per day for the entire school week. Press him a little, but don't set the bar impossibly high so that he is likely to fail. The rebound effect might be more than he can tolerate and he might be reluctant to try next time for fear of being disappointed. It's okay to include small daily rewards and still give out The Big One for long-term success.

Suggestions for Rewards

- *Small Rewards: Videogame or television time, dollar store toys, ice cream, collectable cards or figures, pennies used to "buy" any of the above items.*

- *Big Rewards: Going to a special interest movie, attending a collectable fair, a trip to the dollar store to spend money he has earned for good behavior, purchasing a special toy he has been longing for.*

All of the above tools can ease transitions, lead to more cooperative behavior and generally make our family life more predictable and stable. But what about those times when we've pulled out all the stops and, yet, our child still has a meltdown?

In the following section we'll discuss in detail the different stages of a meltdown and strategies for dealing with them in a way that maintains safety and dignity for all involved.

Meltdown: The Word That Strikes Fear in the Heart of the Asperger Parent

Despite the best thought-out plans, priming and predicting and offers of rewards, sometimes things go awry. Maybe there is an expected challenge your child just cannot overcome, or maybe it's already been such a hectic day for him that he is not capable of being flexible.

These are the times that truly try a parent's patience. However, although your child may have lost his ability to be reasoned with at that moment, you haven't lost *your* reason. It's time to use your most highly attuned Super Parent Powers because you will need them to overcome the moment of the meltdown.

Meltdown Misconception

The first and most important lesson to learn about meltdowns is that the child does not want to have one. Many parents and onlookers have the misconception that the child is "throwing a fit" to get his way. This couldn't be further from the truth. Your child is in extreme distress when he is melting down, and not only is he not under your control, he is not under his own control. You might feel like it's duck-and-cover time, but for him, once the storm hits, there's no escape from the flood of emotions that are ravaging his mind and body. He is trapped. Therefore, have compassion!

Why Do Meltdowns Occur?

Meltdowns can be triggered by a variety of things, but commonly they appear to happen when the child is told to do something he doesn't want to do. While this may be a major trigger, it often masks underlying stressors. For example, it is common for many children with neurological disorders to have a meltdown the moment they arrive home from school. The parent may feel bewildered, wondering what on earth she said or did wrong. The answer is probably nothing. Meltdowns are often caused by pent-up frustration and sensory overload from a very stressful day. By the time the child's hand hits the door, he has had it, as illustrated in the following.

Mom! I'm Home!

Morgan arrives home from school at four, slamming the door behind him. Mom says cheerfully, "Hi, honey, how was your day?" as she leans over to ruffle his hair. Morgan jerks away without answering. She tries again, "I bought the yogurt snacks you like." Morgan grunts and opens the fridge to get a snack. Suddenly he slams it and says, "I don't like yogurt!" Surprised and a little hurt, his mom says, "But you asked me to buy them; you said they were your favorite. Would you like something else?"

As his mom continues to speak, Morgan is becoming redder in the face, and is practically shaking when he yells, "I don't like yogurt!" His mother responds, "Morgan, yes you do. You just asked me for them yesterday." Yelling, "I don't want ANYTHING," Morgan stomps off to his room.

Hoping to find out what's wrong, his mother goes in to check on him. When she opens the door, he screams, "Go away!!" She continues to try to talk with him, but when she is met with growls she says almost instinctively, "Stop doing that!" Morgan starts yelling, "Go away! Go away! Go away!" and pushes things off his dresser onto the floor.

For a moment she considers yelling back in frustration, but instead she takes a deep breath, shuts the door and shakily goes back into the kitchen. Morgan's mom doesn't understand why he is upset. Sometimes she is able to predict a meltdown, but she is confused because she can't figure out what triggered it. She also feels hurt by his anger.

Where Is the Trigger?

Morgan's poor mother is trying her best by greeting her son warmly and offering his favorite snack, what on earth went wrong?

Morgan's mom is the innocent victim in this situation, but so is Morgan. Using a little reasoning, knowing what we know about Asperger Syndrome, what can those of us who view the situation through more experienced eyes guess occurred *before* Morgan arrived home? Something outside of his home, at school, after school, or on the bus, set Morgan off. And/or it could be a combination of the level of stress he is experiencing.

What should parents do when faced with a similar situation? If this delayed meltdown occurs frequently after school, it's time to play detective to find out what is going on before your child comes home.

Discuss it with the school. First, alert the school that there is a problem. Perhaps they have some inkling what might be triggering your child. (See *Building a Relationship with the School* in Chapter 5.) There is always an antecedent to a meltdown; there is a reason. This is an opportunity to problem solve with the school to investigate and find solutions. Communication is key. After all, the same thing can happen in reverse, and the staff will appreciate the insight when it's their turn to deal with a delayed meltdown.

Provide comfort. Create a structure that allows your child time to unwind and decompress before having to meet further expectations. Each child has very different and specific needs. It is important to observe over a period of time what helps your child. More on this in Chapter 6.

Understand the basic tools for dealing with meltdowns. When things are already rocky, you don't want to escalate the situation. Your child is depending on you to manage the situation when things get to this point because he can't do so himself. Many a child has been saved from having a meltdown by parents who understand what is happening and let cooler heads prevail.

Breaking Down the Meltdown: It's About to Blow!

If you are the parent of a child with Asperger Syndrome you know what a meltdown is. No need for explanation! But despite your awareness of the main event, you might have missed the cues leading up to it. Brenda Myles and Jack Southwick refer to this as "the rumbling stage" in the cycle of rage (*Asperger Syndrome and Difficult Moments*, 2005). I often relate these terms to those small tremors that sometimes signal an imminent cataclysmic event such as an earthquake or the eruption of a volcano. Many parents, initially at least, lack the finely tuned instruments to pick up those cues that are screaming, "I'm going to blow!" Sometimes the best you can do is hang on because it has already reached the point of no return.

Signs of the rumbling stage. Each child's warning system sends out a different signal; every child has his own way of telling you, "I'm warning you, I'm starting to fall apart! Back off, slow down." Or, "Help me." However, there are some common themes. Outward signs can include whining, heavy sighing, stomping, moving the body in an agitated and impatient way, or verbal cues such as "I'm bored!" "I don't like it!" or simply, "No!" We know one child who takes off his glasses right before he is about to lose it because he doesn't like the feeling of tears against his lenses. Catching him at that moment has often saved the day.

What should you do when you see the lava beginning to boil? Should you just get out of the way, or is there something you can do? Sometimes you are able to gently snuff out a meltdown before it bursts into flame. It depends on how far your child has escalated. Many parents have found that some of the following techniques work for their children.

1. *Stop talking.* Do not engage in verbal warfare. Your child is no longer listening to you. In fact, the sound of your voice is like throwing gas on the flames. State a request, and if the child is not approachable, take another approach – a quiet, waiting approach. Over time you'll figure out just how far you can push it. Unless you are willing to risk a meltdown, it's better to back off. This isn't "giving in and letting him have his way," this is de-escalating the situation and biding your time until your child can be receptive to you.

2. *Keep expectations low for the moment.* This isn't the time to introduce a new idea or person or to transition somewhere else. Wait. Whatever you're in a hurry to do won't go well if your child is having a meltdown anyway.

3. *Allow your child to be alone if he needs to.* A few minutes or an hour of calm might be all your child needs when he is rumbling. Many children naturally curl up somewhere when they feel upset. Let them stay there as long as they need to. However, it's important to check in on them from time to time. If the child is crying, but offers of comfort are met with a screech, back off.

4. *Depending on the child, provide direct comfort.* Some children do not want anyone to touch them when they are agitated. Others seek being held and comforted during this stage. If they say, "Hold me," by all means, do it! This means your child knows what he needs in order to release his anxiety. Deep pressure, instead of light touching, is usually best, but make sure your child doesn't feel restrained. Practice when he doesn't feel upset to know what feels right.

5. *Remember that your child may not be able to clearly express his needs.* Who hasn't heard, "He's just throwing a fit to get your attention." He might be! And what's wrong with needing attention? If you give him attention before the meltdown, he won't associate having to have a meltdown to get it. Sometimes your presence alone is enough to diffuse the situation.

Laying Blame

It's unfair to characterize all meltdowns and behavior problems as being your fault and suggest that you are somehow lacking in the parenting department. While the days of thinking autism is caused by icebox mothers are long gone, some people still jump to the conclusion that it's the parent's fault somehow. As an AS Parent you'll always be subject to judgmental eyes that will characterize you as anything from "overly indulgent" to "neglectful." Despite all your interventions, loving care and attention, your child will sometimes have a meltdown.

Tools for Support and Coping During the Meltdown

You've done your best, but now the point of no return has been reached; your child has erupted like Mt. St. Helens; he is having a meltdown. Now what?

1. *Only move your child if it is an imminent safety concern.* Unless you are in the middle of the street or in a china shop, stay put! Moving a child while he is having a full-blown meltdown can be very dangerous for you and the child. The adrenaline is pumping through his body, and suddenly you've got The Incredible Hulk on your hands. If you pick him up, he may wrestle out of your grip, and you could drop and injure him. The secondary concern is that he could hurt *you*. In some ways, this can be worse for the child. Although he is unable to process what is happening at the time, if he later realizes he has hurt you, it can be devastating. Our children are out of control when they are melting down, but they do NOT want to hurt us.

2. *Do not try to give your child whatever he was asking for before the meltdown.* This is not because you shouldn't "give in and let him have his way," but because at that point he is unlikely to be able to respond to the object, or process the fact that he even has it. Offer it once early on, but pushing it on him will not stop a meltdown. It may even agitate him further because you are adding to the stimuli his brain can't process at that moment. Once the cycle is full blown, it needs to run its course.

3. *Step back and do not intervene unless your child asks you to.* It is important to understand that a child can rarely express his immediate needs during a meltdown, and even if you comply with his wishes, he probably will not be able to respond positively. Again, your job is not to try to "calm him down" at that point; it is to wait.

4. *If there are others close by, move them.* Well-meaning people may try to step up to help you. Tell them very clearly to stay back. Their presence will only escalate the situation. Some parents have even had business-card-sized cards printed to hand out in public situations saying their child has autism and not to interfere.

5. *Make sure not to escalate your own reactions.* It is extremely difficult to stay calm, not to lose your temper or to feel upset when your child, whom you love best in the world, is falling apart. You will experience a kaleidoscope of emotions from anger, to sadness, to embarrassment (especially if it occurs in public). But remember, if YOU cannot understand his needs, who will? Try to step back and disconnect enough so that you are not caught up in his intense emotions and try to think rationally. This takes practice. Lucky you: If you're like most Asperger Parents, you'll get plenty!

6. *Try not to take it personally.* This is one of the most difficult things for parents. It hurts us when our children are screaming, crying, angry. They might even say something like, "I hate you!" "You're mean!" Or "You don't love me!" These are daggers in every parent's heart. Try thinking of it as a symptom of something that your child HAS, but not who he IS. If your child had the flu, would you blame him for throwing up on you? Of course not; it's beyond his control. A meltdown is sort of like that.

7. *Take this opportunity to step back to observe your child carefully.* Pay attention to what appears to escalate or de-escalate his behavior. Watch how he responds to his environment. Is he able to calm down more quickly when he is at home? Probably. Does he get more agitated in a bright place? Does he respond to sound? If it's quiet, does that help? Take note because this is valuable information for future reference. It's helpful to have a notebook and pen handy, especially when you are just starting to evaluate what triggers your child, but just as important, it makes you feel less helpless.

8. *Do NOT restrain the child.* The concept of restraint is antiquated when it comes to children with AS. It is not only potentially dangerous for you and the child, in the long term it is ineffective. In fact, *it may reinforce future meltdowns.* This is why: Our kids find deep pressure relaxing. If you restrain your AS child during a meltdown, he may initially fight you, followed by "giving up" and relaxing his body, and it seems as though it worked. It did! The child's brain has just learned that in order for his body to receive the deep pressure he craves, he *must* have a meltdown. It's not a conscious choice on the child's part; it is part of his

hard wiring. Understanding this can prevent many future melt-downs. If deep pressure is comforting to your child, provide it *before* the meltdown.

The ONLY exception: If your child is hurting himself or in danger, then, of course, you must protect him, and this may include physical contact. But this does *not* mean tackle and pin him. Use the minimal touch required to keep him from being harmed. This is not for situations such as him kicking a wall. It is for extreme situations such as him trying to bang his head on a concrete wall. A major strategy in preventing this situation is to have a home base, a *safe* location to calm before things reach this crisis point. More on this subject in Chapter 6, *Tools for Creating a Comfortable Home Environment.*

Recovery: Easily Shattered

Congratulations! You have successfully entered the recovery phase of the meltdown. Your child is no longer screaming, crying, kicking; he may appear completely calm. But you're not in the clear yet. There is still lava bubbling under the surface that can re-erupt without much provocation. One of the most significant risks in the beginning phase of recovering from a meltdown is re-escalating the situation by taking things in hand too quickly, thereby rekindling the child's raging.

1. *Approach the child carefully.* I approach my child as I would a wounded animal. He may need your help, but you must move with caution. Let him see you approach, don't startle him to avoid causing an instinctual self-defensive reaction. Such behavior may appear to be intentional aggression, but it is just him telling you, "Back off! I'm still not okay."

2. *Don't push your luck.* This is still not the time to insist on compliance, to lecture or to transition the child to another location or activity. Some of the techniques you may have used in the pre-meltdown phase such as being near, but not talking, may help, but again, use trial and error. Some children do not like to be looked at or touched; others want to be physically held or comforted. Think soothing, quiet, calm. It's not unusual for a child to need to sleep for a while.

Post-Recovery and Wrap-Up: Picking up the Pieces

This is the phase when you are both breathing a sigh of relief. You may look the worse for wear, but you've both survived. The child is exhausted, and you probably are, too. This is the time when you pick up the pieces and try to sort them out. You may think you know what triggered the meltdown, but if your child can give you insight, you might discover that it was over something completely unrelated to what you thought. On the other hand, even if the child otherwise has the skills to express himself, sometimes he might have been so overwhelmed that he has little or no memory of the event.

The following are additional reasons why the wrap-up is so important.

1. *Interpret for your child.* Imagine how you would feel if you experienced something extremely traumatic – emotionally, mentally and physically – and had little or no understanding of what occurred and why, and your memory of it were sketchy. How alarmed would you feel? This is a common experience for children with AS. During the wrap-up you serve as your child's interpreter, explaining the events clearly and carefully and filling in the gaps as best you can.

2. *Clarify, don't accuse.* This is not a time to lecture, scold or criticize, and certainly not to shame. This is an opportunity to create a bridge of understanding, reconnect with your child and build trust. In that connection, it is important to recognize that many children with AS not only have trouble distinguishing emotions in others, but also in themselves. That is, they may be confused about how they felt. Explaining what you saw and experienced helps them understand what their emotions are, and therefore is an essential function of the wrap-up. Example:

    Parent: "You were sad that your toy got broken, weren't you?"

    Child: "Yes, I was sad!"

Parent: "I know you were sad; you cried very hard. I saw your tears. I'm sorry you were sad."

Or:

Parent: "You were so angry that you brother broke your toy, weren't you?"

Child: "Grrrr! I was MAD!"

Parent: "I can see that you're still angry about it. But do you know that he didn't do it on purpose? Are you ready to let him say he's sorry?"

Taboo: When the Child Hits the Parent

What if your child hits you during a meltdown? Parents find it painful to admit their child has hit or hurt them because it's not the usual order of things: It is socially unacceptable, so you can't tell anyone for fear of being criticized for letting your child "get away" with it. If this has happened to you, rest assured you aren't alone.

Depending on your child's age and developmental level, decide on how you want to talk about this with him if it happens. Consider the following as you review and plan to act on the situation.

- *Your child may not remember he did it. Again, in those highly charged moments the child may not be able to think clearly, or remember what happened. He might react with surprise when you bring it up, with no memory of what happened. Or his memory might be sketchy.*

- *Are you interpreting it correctly? Did he purposely swing and hit you, or was he flailing randomly and accidentally hit you? There is a huge difference. If it was accidental, there is little reason to mention it. If you believe he hit you with intent, he might have no understanding that he actually hurt you. Explain very carefully to him that grown-ups hurt, too. Give an example of a time when he was hurt, "Remember when you fell and hurt your arm? That's what it feels like when you hurt me."*

- *Review carefully what you might have done to inadvertently contribute to the child physically acting out toward you during a meltdown.* During this highly charged emotional outburst, a child easily feels threatened and therefore is instinctually defensive. For example, he may interpret any attempt at reaching toward him, getting into his personal space and, certainly, grabbing him, as a threatening attack, and therefore try to protect himself. Your child is reacting instinctually; he is not thinking. Removing others, keeping clear of your child's flailing and stepping back from his aggressive posture can prevent most, if not all, hits from landing, or possibly from being conceived in the first place.

- *Decide whether to bring up the hitting at all.* This is especially true if your child's self-esteem is extremely fragile and bringing it up at all will overly shame, or even devastate him. Another option is to wait for a future, more stable time when there is some distance from the event to speak with him about it.

Teach Forgiveness by Example

Our kids often feel terrible when they realize they've hurt us and may secretly carry guilt, which is further damaging to their self-esteem. Make sure your child knows that you forgive him when he makes a mistake, whether intentional or not. If he is able to remember and understand what he has done, tell him about your feelings.

Parent: "Do you remember hitting me when you were having a meltdown?"

Child: "Yes. But I didn't mean to!"

Parent: "I know you didn't, sweetheart. Do you feel sad that you hit me?"

Child: "I don't know."

Parent: "It makes me sad when you hit me and it also hurts. But I'm sorry that you were so upset. I feel sad when you're hurting, too."

The child may react with remorse, anger, sadness. Or he may not seem to react with clear emotions. If you can help him discuss how he feels, it will help him have a greater understanding how you feel, and how others feel.

What About MY Feelings When My Child Strikes out at Me?

It is incredibly painful to have your child hurt you physically, but it hurts even more emotionally. If it happens publicly, you might feel embarrassed as you sense the shocked eyes of others judge both you and your child. This hurts. But perhaps it is when parents are alone that the hurt becomes more intensified. You may be filled with self-blame about how you handled the specific situation, or in general about your feelings of failure as a parent. You may worry about your child's future, fearing that as he gets bigger he might actually seriously harm you, himself or others. These are but a few of the thoughts that might run through your mind after such a charged emotional experience. It is important to take care of yourself during those times. In fact, it is important to take care of yourself PERIOD.

Phone a friend. Call on your community of support when you are flooded with self-doubts and recriminations. It's important to get emotional support and to discharge some of the emotions you are feeling. You need comfort from those who care about you. It's important to seek this help from people who understand, such as other AS Parents.

Take care of your body. Your mind and body have been through a great deal of stress during your child's meltdown, and adding physical blows increases the feelings of vulnerability. Don't immediately charge into action and onto the next task. Do things that help you relax: take a bath, a drive, a nap, if possible. Don't forget to eat. Let yourself unwind, or just as your child can re-escalate, you'll find yourself zooming up on the stress scale very quickly. Get a good night's rest and then tomorrow you'll take on the world again.

Wake up and take charge. Now that you are of a clear and rested mind, you can assess the situation and make decisions. It's time to ask yourself some questions, such as:

* *"Is this an ongoing pattern?"* If you are getting hurt often, then it's time to look for the underlying causes. If you are unsure what the triggers are, it's time to play detective and look for patterns.

- *"Do I need more help?"* If you are unable to figure out where to go from here, perhaps it's time to seek professional guidance. It's okay to say you need help; we all do. More on the importance of this in Chapter 4.

Discussing all of these emotional issues is difficult, and it is a delicate time for both of you. While you may have your own feelings to deal with, remember you are the parent. It is your job to set aside your own emotional needs at the moment of crisis to help your child. This does not mean you put off these needs forever. It just means that for now you must keep your focus on your child. When he has recovered, *you need to recover, too.* This is why it is so important to have long-term plans for taking care of yourself in order to remain patient, healthy and to prevent burn-out. This will give you a fuller inner reserve to meet your child's needs during those difficult moments, as discussed in more detail in Chapter 3.

Scrapbook-Worthy Day

My husband and I have an odd reaction to our children's outbursts on occasion. Sometimes we laugh. It's either laugh or cry, and laughing feels a whole lot better. With summer vacation ending we thought a day devoted to the "kidlets" would be just the ticket. We took them for a rare outing to Hometown Buffet, where they loaded up on their favorite bland food: mashed potatoes, macaroni and cheese and chicken. All of this pretty much tastes the same, but that, of course, is the appeal in the first place. After lunch, we headed for what might have been the worst movie I've ever suffered through for the sake of my children to date, **Yu-gi-oh.**

Our oldest, Tom, wasn't sure he would be able to tolerate the sound despite the earplugs, so he sat on my lap with his head buried in my chest. At 12, he is almost as tall as I am, but luckily for me and my tingling legs, Special Interest won out, and he eventually slipped into his own seat. All three kids were so mesmerized for the entire hour and a half that at one point I considered holding a mirror under their noses to see if they were still breathing. I thought, "Gee, why don't we take them out more often? They are doing great!"

While my husband wisely slept through the movie, my mind drifted as I pictured the scrapbook page I'd like to create with the movie tickets as mementos so we could always remember this special day. Obviously, we don't get out much! Then, as we left the mall, I was reminded why we stay home.

As we exited the theater, we passed a bank of gumball-type machines, and since the kids had been so good all day, we dug down for quarters. That was our downfall! Kito and Kaede bought the first thing they could lay their hands on. Tom spent 10 minutes carefully studying each and every machine while we wrangled the other two and tried not to get too impatient. Finally, he stuffed two quarters into the only machine he wanted something from … and it jammed. Hopelessly, irrevocably jammed.

We desperately tried to salvage the situation, but it was too late. The loss of a 50-cent toy instantly demolished all memories of 60 dollars worth of a happy, calm family day once and for all (dinner/movie for five people). Tom went into a screaming/sobbing mode. Overload. He sank to the floor crying, and we gently helped him up and began walking him out. Passively he allowed this until we reached the exit, then he screamed, "You're hurting me! I am not going with you!" Groan. All eyes on the child kidnappers and/or child-beating parents. We pretty much expected mall security to show up, but apparently a child shrieking in agony is either not an unusual occurrence or they were on a donut break.

So, I sat on the floor and held and comforted my son as people stepped around us until he was a moveable boy again. Then we carefully led him out to the car wailing all the way (him, that is, not me, although I felt like it!). On the way home all three children cried loudly. Tom was howling, "I'm not happy!" and the other two did back-up in stereo, "He's hurting my ears!" My husband and I caught each other's eyes in the rearview mirror and, heaven help us, we just started laughing so hard we were crying! I have no idea why we thought this was funny. Perhaps we were struck by the irony: Over the years we have come to realize that the amount of money we spend on the children for fun and leisure seems to be in direct proportion to how badly they behave afterwards. So, once again, it was laugh or cry, and since we felt like both, we did! There's no place like home, but failing that, *next time we'd better stick to my one-or-two transitions rule. That third one's always the death knell for family outings.*

I could share many stories of outings that were absolutely idyllic. We do have them! But it's important for us as parents to understand that meltdowns happen despite our best intentions, preparations and parenting skill level. If there is one gift I could give you, it is to know that whether it was something beyond your control, or whether you inadvertently contributed to it in some way, a meltdown is not your fault. You are doing the best you can, and so is your child. Go with it. And try to find some small nugget in those moments – even if it is to enjoy the relief when it's over. Then let it go.

Things to Take with You

- *Child's Medication: Extra in case you can't make it home on schedule*
- *Headache Medicine: For you! No need for explanation, is there?*
- *Earplugs: To help your child tolerate noisy social situations. It won't entirely block his hearing, but it will decrease the intensity*
- *Emergency Contact Numbers: The doctor, the school, your best friend or other family contact*
- *Boredom-Proof Bag O'Tricks: Handheld games, walkman or small radio, snacks*
- *Paper and Pen: For cartooning or creating a social narrative (visual aid) on the spot*
- *Rewards: Pennies, tickets or tokens, candy, cards*
- *Rose-Colored Glasses: To see the world through a lovely filter of optimism*
- *Your Self-Renewing Well of Patience: The more you use, the more you'll have*
- *A Bucketful of Compassion: Apply liberally to child and self*
- *Magic Invisibility Cloak: Or wear your thick-skinned, criticism-proof anti-embarrassment cape*
- *Your Sense of Humor: If none of the above works, then this is what you'll need the most!*

Chapter 3

One Pie, Too Many Slices!

Tools for Meeting Everyone's Needs

The needs in the Asperger Family are diverse and can be overwhelming. It may seem as though there is not enough time in the day to meet everyone's needs. People look at my life and ask me, "How do you do so many things?" On a "good" day, I say, "Momentum." On a "bad" day, I respond matter-of-factly, "I don't do all of them well." Something has to be sacrificed, but preferably, not the family members themselves. I often feel like a pie that only has so many slices, and everyone wants one. Where's my slice?

This chapter is about why you should cut yourself both a little slack and a bigger sliver of the pie than you've probably been treating yourself to. How *do* we equitably divide the family resources so it's fair for everyone? First by understanding what those needs are, and then by making them a priority.

Taking Care of Yourself

As a parent, your hands are full. You have too many things to do, money is often tight, and everyone in your life needs or wants something from you. If time, money, resources are already limited, who is inevitably the last person on your list? You.

Most parents push their own needs to the bottom of the list and almost never get that far. Maybe we don't get there on purpose, because we think we should put our children above all else. There is merit to that line of thinking, after all we've all heard about parents

who don't make their kids a priority, and the disastrous results that can lead to. It's just that many parents take it to extremes. They don't allow anything for themselves. Why should you put yourself higher on your list of priorities than you probably are? Because it's not selfish to take care of yourself. On the contrary, it's selfish NOT to.

Have you ever thought about the message behind the flight attendant's safety presentation before take-off? "Please place the oxygen mask over your own face before assisting your child." Why? Because if you don't and you pass out, who will take care of your child? There may be a larger lesson here: Taking care of yourself *is* taking care of your family.

Parenting is the hardest job in the world, and caring for a child with special needs brings added worries, concerns and duties. You cannot afford to burn out. You must take care of yourself or you'll be cheating your child and your family out of your ability to care for them. Do you ever feel like the walking dead – wiped out, exhausted, overwhelmed? How effective are you as a caretaker, advocate and loving parent when you are like that? You think you're tired now, how about another 20 years of this? Or more? How long can you realistically put your own needs off without it taking a toll on everybody in your family? So if you love them, which you do, you will take care of YOU.

So What Does This Mean for You?

You're thinking about it, aren't you? It makes sense that you must take care of you so you can take care of your family, but what's the next step?

Give yourself permission. It sounds simple, but it is probably the biggest factor in whether parents take care of themselves or not. If you need permission from someone else: I'm giving it to you!

Take stock. Look around, something's got to go. Maybe it's just an expectation you put on yourself more than an actual thing.

Lower your expectations. It's not often you get this advice! In this case, it means lowering some of the ridiculously unreasonable expectations you have of what you are supposed to accomplish in one day. It's okay to let the laundry sit in the basket for a while, or have your family eat off paper plates.

Care for yourself. You care for everyone in your family. Who takes care of you? Maybe *just* you. So, if you don't, who will? This includes "simple" but hard-to-do-things like taking care of your body such as sleeping and eating well, and more difficult things like scheduling time for yourself.

Schedule it or it won't happen. Pick up the phone, put something on the calendar, or months slip by without you doing anything for you.

Enlist cohorts in crime. Okay, it's not a crime, but it almost feels as though you and your friends are up to some kind of mischief when you are doing something delightfully indulgent such as laughing while having a piece of cheesecake and a cup of coffee together. It's healthy mischief! Friends who take care of themselves help you take care of yourself, too. Be a good influence on each other.

What Does It Mean for Your Family?

Let's say that you have decided to make yourself a priority. It's not like you can put your family on hold, so what happens now? Somebody else has to pick up the slack a little. Whether it is enlisting more support from your spouse, or insisting he help out more, the chores must become a little more evenly distributed. Sometimes this means a spouse, at other times it means having your children be a little more independent. It may also mean depending on others outside your family for support to lessen your burden, particularly if you are a single parent. See Chapter 4, *Tools for Building a Community of Support*.

Guess what? Not everyone is going to be thrilled at this turn of events. Things might get a little uncomfortable for you and your family as you all make the adjustment to a more balanced life. But think of what your family gains in return – a living, breathing, happier parent. A parent who is healthy and, ultimately, more physically and emotionally available for her family. Remember, "If Mama ain't happy, ain't nobody happy!"

Burning the Candle at Both Ends

There are times when I don't just burn the candle at both ends; I burn it in the middle. And just about the time I've almost melted into a puddle of wax, I get sick. Do I take to my bed and rest? In a perfect world, yes, but like many other things, I just can't quite get it right. This is what happened LAST time.

Dextrometherphen is apparently Latin for: No sleep all night. It also means that you will wake up three hours after taking it, feeling as though you have taken 10 No-Doze downed with a gallon of coffee. And you will suddenly have attention deficit disorder so even though you're awake, you won't be able to complete a rational thought. So you'll lie in bed for hours trying to remember what day it is, followed by attempting to make a grocery list before remembering that you already went grocery shopping TODAY, followed by thinking, "What was I just thinking about?" Followed by "What day is it? And what do I need to buy at the store?" AGAIN. Then you hope to manage to keep your faculties about you tomorrow so you remember NOT to take Dextrometherphen and repeat this nightmare tomorrow night.

It isn't until I wake up in the morning that I realize that I say that EVERY year after taking this cold remedy. But it must wipe out long-term memory or something because I don't remember that fact until after I've taken it AGAIN. Note to self: Stick with chamomile tea with honey.

Maybe someone else will maintain their memory cells and remind me not to take cold medicine NEXT year. Or somebody will need to remind me next week because I might have already forgotten by then. Or tomorrow. Or today. Wait a minute, what was I just talking about? And what day is it? Where's my grocery list?

Obviously this was a case of me not taking care of myself and consequently being less productive at my Mom job. But I've pulled out the tools and made some adjustments to fix that. Although I can't always help it if I get sick, I hardly think it's a coincidence that last year before I started taking better care of myself, I was sick at least a half a dozen times. This year I've made my health, my life and my well-being a priority. I've been sick ONCE. Coincidence? I think not. And the side effect of that? As it turns out, I have MORE time to spend with my family, not less.

Sharing Territory with Dad

Why is it that moms are usually more actively involved with our AS kids? Perhaps it continues to be the cultural norm for mothers to fall into the nurturing role, and many of us moms see that as our primary identity. And c'mon let's admit it, as moms we are sometimes not willing to let dads do "our" job. We worry they won't do it "right." But sharing the parental load doesn't mean we have to give it up entirely; it just means leveling the load. Perhaps we should move over and give dads a chance to help out and get more involved. Or even insist that they do. And why isn't HE insisting in the first place?

Dig Deeper: What's Really Going on with Dad?

Is it simply a case of slacking off and letting Mom do everything? Or is there something going on under the surface that your spouse is not sharing with you, or that perhaps he doesn't even quite understand himself?

Dad may feel inadequate. If Mom is spending more time with the kids and has undoubtedly developed skills to take care of them, it often seems just "easier" to let Mom do it all. Because when he *does* fill in, Dad doesn't have the same arsenal of skills and feels overwhelmed.

Dads have different priorities in mind. Even when both parents work, it often seems it is the dad who focuses most on the financial aspect of helping the family. It's been a long time since man was clubbing the dinosaur to bring it home for dinner, but sometimes guys still seem to be in that mode of thinking. Dad may view his financial commitment toward the family as the only thing he has to offer, and in AS families the reality is there is often a pressing financial need.

Dad may be carrying a load of grief of his own. As sad as this is, even nowadays dads may not feel they can express their emotions as readily as moms. They might believe they have to be strong for their family, and may perceive showing how much they are hurting as "weakness." Dads like to "fix" things, and this isn't something they can readily fix. Dad might be depressed and withdrawn. Or, he might look angry. He's not angry at the mom and kids, he's angry because he feels helpless. He may be throwing himself wholeheartedly into working even harder to support his family to escape dealing with those feelings. But in the long term is this healthy for the family?

Give Dad Tools for the Job

Dads like tools! It's a concept that they can relate to. Dad may not realize his full potential, so it's up to Mom to "encourage" him by providing the tools and supports he needs to get the job done.

Provide visual supports. Dads are often visual creatures. They like to SEE what it is you are talking about because this is how their brains work. Like for your kids, draw them a picture. Literally. The picture schedule doesn't just help the child, it can take the mystery out of the job for Dad.

Give clear instructions. Any person who isn't in the regular routine of taking care of a child with AS can be overwhelmed about what to do. Just because it's a "duh" factor for you, doesn't mean it is for everyone else. Providing clear instructions that eliminate having to think or make decisions under stress is better for everyone. A list on the fridge is worth a hundred explanations. It's fine for Dad to make dinner while you're out, but how about posting a menu so he doesn't have to come up with it on his own? At least until he gets the hang of it. Keep it simple to increase the odds of success!

Back off a little. This is the hard part for moms. There is a learning curve involved as dads pick up the tools and develop the skills to handle things in our absence. We worry that dads won't do "our" job as well as we do. Maybe they will; maybe they won't. But odds are that everyone will survive. And eventually they'll get better at it.

Accept that Dad brings his own "style" to the table. In most cases dads do not do things the same way moms do. And that's good! As mothers we are more likely to wrap our children up in cotton, especially when they have special needs; we provide the softness and comfort. Dads, in general, are rough and tumble and take more risks. Combining the two tends to bring balance to the family.

One of the hardest things for us as moms is to let go of some of the control and let Dad and other adults take some responsibility for our kids. But in holding on to our control too tightly, we may, in fact, be shortchanging our kids in the long run. Children who are lucky enough to have *at least* two loving adults (and hopefully even more!) involved in their lives are more likely to succeed. Our AS kids, like all children, need to know that Mom is not the only person on the planet who can meet their needs. They must develop close and trusting relationships with other people in their lives.

This will initially be hard on Mom, who is used to being the primary caregiver, but eventually we learn to enjoy the sense of relief when we allow someone else to share the joys and responsibilities of caring for our child.

What's in it for you, Dad? First of all, your wife will not be staring daggers at you when you walk in the door, and she'll be oh-so-appreciative, which is always a good thing. You'll feel better too because you'll feel more competent and sure of yourself with your kids.

It is the beginning stage of building a community of support, starting at home. This benefits your child, your family and you, Mom! And to those dads who attend IEP meetings and conferences, read books and, most important, take an active role in their child's life – good for you! You are a rare gift, and your child will greatly benefit from your involvement and your entire family will be healthier. And Mom, once you build some trust in Dad's ability to handle things – even if not exactly the way you do them – it frees you up to take better care of yourself.

The "F" Word

I used the "F" word several times today. "F" as in Father. *I said to my Constant Interruptions, er, I mean* children, *"Go ask your FATHER." My frustrated husband said, "Arrg! I don't know what to do with them!" I laughed and said, "Well, let me finish writing this book, then you can read it and find out!"*

Despite our constant reinforcement and explanations, our children often get stuck on the idea that only Mom can make a peanut butter and jelly sandwich "just right" (no crust!), wipe a tear while bandaging skinned knees and listen to their list of Yu-gi-oh cards and Legos they intend to collect in the future. I've spent so many years paying attention to my children's needs that I can almost do it on autopilot. In the short term it's often easier to just get my fanny off the couch and do it myself, yet I continue to reinforce the message to the children that Dad is capable. And just as important, it also teaches Dad he is capable! To do otherwise would in the long run be cheating my family out of a more richly rewarding life of trusting that other people can meet their needs, and eventually they can meet their own needs! At least that's the story I'm telling my husband. Do you think he'll buy it?

Marriage: Where's My Fairy Tale Ending?

While the divorce rate for the general population in the United States has hovered around 50% for a number of years, the statistics for divorce are reported as high as 85% for parents of children with autism. This is alarming, but sadly not that surprising for parents who live as we do. It is often said that the two things couples fight about most are money and children. Having a child with autism heightens the intensity of emotions regarding both of those issues. The following are a few of the questions that AS parents are faced with that can lead to conflict.

Where Does the Money Go?

We must make so many decisions regarding our child's well-being, and money is tightly wound up within it. Do we decide to spend ourselves into debt pursuing every avenue to treat our child? Do we pursue alternative treatments that our insurance will not cover and go into debt if necessary? When parents do not agree, it can be a firestorm because the stakes are so high.

Does One Parent Stay Home?

Two-parent families may opt to have one parent stay home to meet the increased needs of the child, such as driving to therapy, getting medical treatment, being more involved in school, battling for services, etc. Or, conversely, if one parent has been staying at home, but the financial burden has gotten heavier, is there disagreement about whether the second parent should work or not?

What About Our Time?

There is so little of it! Do we no longer go out or have time away together because the child's needs are so great and we don't trust anyone else to care for him? And then, do we feel neglected by our spouse? Do we feel alone? *Resentful?*

How Do We Make Significant Decisions?

What if parents disagree on any of the above, who has the final say, and what if there is no way to compromise?

So, Are We Doomed?

There are no easy answers to any of these questions, nor is the prognosis good for marriages that are coping with the extra concerns of being an Asperger Family. But statistics are general; they are not necessarily *your* family. The stress is enormous, but many families have found greater strength in facing adversity together. One of the keys to prevent burnout and, consequently loss of relationships, is to keep a little something for yourself so you have something more to give each other *and* your child. Because as they say, a chain is only as strong as its weakest link. You all must be healthy and strong as individuals to stay connected.

I See Red

The weekend is a time when (theoretically) I can step back, let my husband, Nobuo, take on more parental responsibility and focus on other projects. My idea of "watching" the kids is to use my actual eyes ON the children, but my husband has a different approach. His idea of "watching" is that unless someone is screaming, then all is well, so he might as well see what's on ESPN. Recently on one such day I had ensconced myself on the living room sofa in full view so I could easily witness potential life-threatening mishaps as I tapped away at my laptop, headphones ear-damaging loud to block out the sound of the children chattering like screeching monkeys as they ran through the house like a herd of buffalo. But there was the assumption that the man of the house was minding the store while I was partially checked out. Here's what happened.

Me: tap, tap, tap on the keyboard. I see a soccer ball go flying through the dining room from the kitchen (of course, where else would it come from?). It wasn't the soccer ball that tipped me off to trouble brewing. While it's true that I don't have balls flying all over the house every day, it was the speed at which it flew. I pulled off my headphones and was just about to investigate when Kito, our 10-year-old, ran past me at breakneck speed, and out the sliding glass door … into the rain … in his underpants.

Okay, we can't have THAT! I stepped out onto the deck and pulled him inside. I flailed about trying to shut the door with my foot, as I struggled to block my son's exit. At the same time the other children came running in, both loudly trying to explain what had just happened, while my requests to (A) "Shut the door please!" and (B) "Get your father!" were ignored. Then I noticed out of the corner of my eye the blinking **red** light on my laptop. Oh no, the battery! I'd been writing for over an hour and hadn't saved it. Completely overwhelmed, I hollered, "Nobuo, I need help! Nobuo!" A minute passed, two minutes, three. Meanwhile, laptop: blink, blink, blink. Kids: "Mama!" Kito: "Wah!" And me: "Nobuo!"

Kito is getting more worked up at the sound of my voice, he's wiggling around me trying to dodge out the door, and I'm becoming frantic. I shriek, "NOBUO!" a few more times. Finally, my husband arrives on the scene. I'm yelling, "Come help me!" while my hair is practically standing on end. I'm obviously visibly distressed. Does he pick up the pace? Nope! He meanders across the living room, strolls casually up to me and asks calmly, "What?" I was pretty keyed up and hollered a little louder than I needed to at that point, considering he was now a foot from me instead of on the other side of the house (what can I say, I don't have a quick-adjusting volume control), "Watch Kito for a second!" And I dove for the laptop like sliding into homebase, pushed "save" and darted right back just in time to nab Kito, who was halfway out the door already. My husband hadn't moved a muscle; he was staring at me incredulously. Kito mercifully started to calm down and crawled under the beanbag chair to decompress. By then, boy, did I want to join him!

Did I mention what I'd been writing when this event occurred? I was in the middle of the "Marriage" section above, and had just added the subtitle, "So, Are We Doomed?" You have no idea how tempted I was to simply write, "Yes." In spite of the drama and how obvious it is from this story where both my husband's and my own shortcomings are, when cooler heads prevail we DO understand our needs, both as individuals and as a family. We're on the same page, and between the two of us, we find balance. Our system: Only one parent is allowed to freak out at a time. Remarkably effective!

"Don't Forget Me!" – Siblings

We've taken time to reflect on your experience as parents and the perspective of the AS child. Now we will focus on the child in your family who may be hurting the most, your neurotypical child. Why may she be suffering? Because she may not entirely understand what is happening in her family. She may not have the words to express her feelings. As a child she does not have access to the coping mechanisms a free-willed adult does. Therefore, just as it is our responsibility to advocate for our AS child, we must also be thinking of our neurotypical child's needs.

Don't misplace your patience when it comes to your neurotypical child. Have you ever felt as though you do not have an ounce of patience left? Has your AS child already pushed you beyond your limit and now one more thing finally sends you over the edge? It's happened to all of us. Logically, we know that we cannot take it out on the AS child, and we try not to. But then your NT child bursts in or acts up and you snap, "Cut it out! Can't you see I've already got my hands full?!" Oops. BIG oops. How can you help your NT child feel as important and help her have her own needs met? First a little insight into her world.

Your NT child may be keeping it to herself. Whether or not you've uttered the fateful statement above, she may already recognize that you are too busy or distracted to help her. Or she may not think her own needs are important enough to be met because from outside appearances they pale in comparison to the struggles her AS sibling faces.

Not all is as it seems. Acting out is a sign that many people recognize as the behavior of a child who is asking for more attention. But what about when you have a "perfect" child who does the opposite? She may get praised for being "easy," "good," "well behaved" and "No trouble at all!" She might be a super-achiever and has adopted this identity as her way of getting attention. The perfect child can often be in as much pain as the child who is rebelling.

So how do you know if your other child has painful feelings associated with her sibling's Asperger Syndrome? First, *assume* the sibling needs attention just as much as the AS child regardless of whether she shows it or not. Just as you have learned to think ahead to meet your AS child's needs, it's important to foresee what your neurotypical child may need long term.

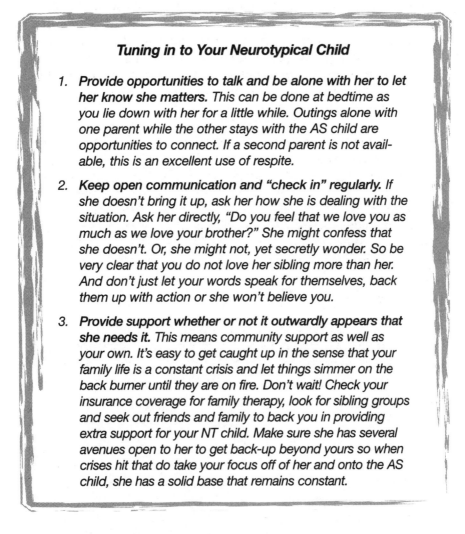

Tuning in to Your Neurotypical Child

1. *Provide opportunities to talk and be alone with her to let her know she matters. This can be done at bedtime as you lie down with her for a little while. Outings alone with one parent while the other stays with the AS child are opportunities to connect. If a second parent is not available, this is an excellent use of respite.*

2. *Keep open communication and "check in" regularly. If she doesn't bring it up, ask her how she is dealing with the situation. Ask her directly, "Do you feel that we love you as much as we love your brother?" She might confess that she doesn't. Or, she might not, yet secretly wonder. So be very clear that you do not love her sibling more than her. And don't just let your words speak for themselves, back them up with action or she won't believe you.*

3. *Provide support whether or not it outwardly appears that she needs it. This means community support as well as your own. It's easy to get caught up in the sense that your family life is a constant crisis and let things simmer on the back burner until they are on fire. Don't wait! Check your insurance coverage for family therapy, look for sibling groups and seek out friends and family to back you in providing extra support for your NT child. Make sure she has several avenues open to her to get back-up beyond yours so when crises hit that do take your focus off of her and onto the AS child, she has a solid base that remains constant.*

The Comparison Game

We automatically think about not making the AS child "feel bad" by making comparisons about how further advanced his neurotypical sibling is, but are we missing the opportunity to praise the NT child in

the process? It is all right to pull your children aside and praise their accomplishments individually, whatever they are. The point is for all children to reach *their* full potential. They should feel good about what THEY can do, aside from their siblings. This is a healthy message parents should always convey to their children – "We are proud of you for doing the best *you* can."

Resentment

Some siblings feel resentful at having to "grow up" too quickly when they have a brother or sister with a disability. While it's true that having to assume responsibility and learning that life isn't always a cake walk is a long-term beneficial lesson, it is not something you should force on the NT sibling. She will have many hard knocks as a result of her family's struggles, so do whatever you can to shield her from adult responsibilities too early in life.

Do not put her in charge of caring for a sibling with Asperger Syndrome. If you are having trouble meeting his needs, feeling frustrated with his behavior and generally overwhelmed, remember your neurotypical child will have similar feelings. The big difference is that you are an adult and this is *your* child. Never fall for the temptation to put the NT child into the parental role. It isn't fair.

Provide her with her own space. Just as the AS child needs a quiet hide-a-way of his own to decompress, this is equally true for the NT child. She may feel overwhelmed at the constant stress of her sibling's meltdowns. AS children may also be destructive, and the sib should be provided with the security of not having her possessions destroyed. Therefore, if at all possible, she needs her own room. *Note:* Don't forget to go in periodically and check on your neurotypical child, particularly after any major incident. This is an important opportunity to allow her to express her feelings.

Do not tell her, "I understand how you feel." You don't, unless you also grew up with a sibling with Asperger Syndrome. You can have empathy, you can listen, but don't assume you know how she feels.

Reassure your NT child that she will not have to be responsible for her sibling when she is an adult. Even if you have never expressed to her that he will become her responsibility, she may worry that he will. Tell her that she is allowed to dream of whatever she wants to become, apart from her sibling. Her life is her own.

Foster her separate identity. If she is allowed to pursue her own interests and develop a separate identity, she is less likely to feel forced to run from the family fold in order to create one. Asperger Syndrome will always be a part of your lives as parents, but the NT sibling will eventually choose whether or not to continue to be involved. Ultimately, it is her decision to be close to her AS sibling once she is an adult.

Recognize she may be grieving, too. As adults we have a broader range of experiences; children only know their own reality. Neuro-typical siblings are also grieving the loss of the kind of sibling they can never have. They may even idealize what it would be like to have a neurotypical sibling, just as we carry the image of a post-card-perfect family in our minds. They too are grieving the loss of what will never be.

A Word About Family Resources

Your NT child may be well aware that important resources are being spent on her sibling's medical needs, for example. She probably knows because she's overheard conversations, or sometimes been told directly, "We can't afford it because we have to pay for your brother's therapy, medication," etc. While this is stating a fact, it is a burden that a child should not have to carry. She might feel guilty for using the resources that she gets. Or she may resent or blame her AS sibling because she thinks she doesn't get what she wants because of him.

Be careful what you say in front of your NT child. She should not carry adult worries such as money. Find the balance. For example, you can say, "I'm sorry, we can't afford that." Or, "That's a "want" not a "need." Teach her the difference. It's not good for kids to get every-thing they want anyway, but don't lay the blame on the doorstep of your AS child, or it may affect the family dynamic in a negative way.

Offer plenty of opportunities for your NT child to be involved in activities on her own, but continue to provide your support and encouragement. It is important to set aside funds and time for your NT child *even if it means you have to sacrifice something else, including occasionally something for your child with AS.* You love all of your children, regardless of what their abilities are, and while your AS child will have greater needs in some areas, that doesn't mean he should come first all the time. That isn't fair to anyone.

Recently a mother of a child with Asperger Syndrome was lamenting how much he and his sister fight. Almost in the next breath she said, "His AS has nothing to do with *her*." It's easy to overlook that even as our child's Asperger Syndrome affects us, it affects everyone around him, especially a sibling. And just as we learn to look at our AS child with eyes of understanding, we need to do the same for our neurotypical child. We must address her needs because we are also *her* advocate in the world. She needs us and our support.

Inexpensive Ways to Take Care of Yourself

We often think of going out, or doing things for ourselves, as taking too much time or resources away from our families. We may believe it's an all-or-nothing proposition, but that's often because our "me" tank has been running on empty way too long and we feel SO in need of a fill. But if you have regularly scheduled times for yourself, you might find that you don't feel the desperation to stay out as long, your tank fills up quicker and won't need to be "topped off" as often. If you make yourself a priority on a regular basis, you will pull fewer resources away from your family, not more. The intention is not to do all of the items on the following list. Choose one or two that suit you. If one doesn't work out, try another. Don't underestimate the power of small things incorporated on a regular basis (this is key) to recharge and rejuvenate you.

- *Make the bathroom your sanctuary.* At our house the bathroom is sacred. No one is allowed to bother parents in the bathroom. Yes, they still stick their fingers under the door when you're in the bathtub, but you can pretend not to notice (earplugs or headphones!). Stock it with music, candles (and maybe a secret stash of chocolate, shhh!). The bathroom can also be your sneaky escape for speaking on the phone or reading a book without interruptions. Even 15 minutes can make a difference in recharging your batteries for the rest of the evening.

- *Go for a walk.* This is a simple and effective way to burn off stress. For added enjoyment ask a neighbor to go with you. You can become refreshed and full of juicy gossip. Besides, when you make plans to include somebody else, you are less likely to cancel.

- *Go for a drive.* Feeling like you've reached your limit? Even if you have nowhere in mind to go, leave the kids with your spouse for an hour and just drive around the neighborhood. There is even something soothing about driving around in the dark unwinding for a while. If you're lucky, your spouse will have put the kids to bed while you're gone. Then you can give him/her a little extra special attention to show your gratitude.

- *Go to a flower nursery.* You don't have to spend a great deal of money. You can buy a single flower and have your kids help you plant it. If you don't have any yard space, find a container somewhere. Even an herb plant in your kitchen window is fun. No container? Be creative. Go to the dollar store. Think small.

- *Visit the library.* Many of us love to read, but it can get expensive. A trip to the library is just the ticket. Grab the bestsellers. If you're in a hurry, this is a good way to try new things you might not otherwise choose. When you have more time to linger, stroll the aisle for unexpected treasures.

- *Go bargain hunting.* Like bargains? If you haven't tried secondhand shopping from discount stores such as St. Vincent de Paul/Goodwill/Salvation Army, give it a try. If you're not interested in the clothes, then how about some cheap books? Who can't use a stack of Harlequin romance novels for 10 cents each? Or a flower pot to plant that lovely herb for your kitchen window!

- *Go out for coffee.* As mentioned, many of us tend to think that if we go out, it has to be for a long time. That's probably in part due to having reached a major stress level and then not wanting to go home! If you have a regular outing planned with friends even once a month (better yet, once a week), you'll look forward to it with great anticipation. And eventually you won't feel the intense need to stretch it out because there is always next week. If your friends are all busy, go anyway. Have a date with yourself and one of the books you found at the library.

- *Schedule 15 minutes a day with your spouse.* This is harder than it sounds, but well worth it. Having a regular schedule in the evening for your kids will ensure you can make time for your husband or wife with fewer interruptions. Perhaps it's during their favorite TV show, or you may divert their attention with a DVD. You might need to talk about the kids, but don't forget the importance of your relationship with your spouse. Share your day, and be sympathetic to each other's stresses. Some parents find the best use of their time is to snuggle or otherwise be close, oops, uh, I meant, talk about very serious matters! Seriously though, sneaking time to "bond" is extremely important.

- *Get respite and date your spouse.* Or get creative. How about taking a massage class together? Or how about just going dancing? When was the last time you did that? In the summer, pack a picnic lunch, grab a blanket and just "be" together; there are often free concerts in the park. Remember what you did B.C. (Before Children)? It's all right for you to have a relationship with your spouse that has nothing to do with the kids!!

You Might Just Be an Asperger Family If . . .

- There are more than 25 books about the same subject in your home

- You carry earplugs in your purse "just in case"

- None of your clothes has tags

- Someone suggesting you pick something up at Wal-Mart sends shivers of terror down your spine

- The words "nerdy engineer type" describes either you or your husband

- The principal groans when you enter the school and makes a hasty exit

- You understand the following abbreviations: AS, ASD, SPED, IEP, OT and GFCF. (Bonus points if you also know PT, D.D. and SSI)

- Your child's school file is more than two inches thick

- You've ever had to explain why your child is pinching his nose shut and trying to run away and/or have had to apologize for comments like "Eww, she stinks!"

- When you go out with your child, you either get sympathetic or dirty looks (which further reinforces your lack of eye contact policy)

- The most common compliment you get is, "Gee, you're awfully patient"

- Even your skeptical relatives begin to think there really is "something wrong" with your child

- **Sign up for a class by yourself.** It's not very expensive to take a class from the local recreation center or community college. One night a week away among other adults discussing something besides autism can be intellectually stimulating. You can also be more serious about it and take a credit course, or be equally serious about just having fun by taking a pottery or an art class. Finances tight? Look in the community pages of your local newspaper for groups and classes that are free. Join a choir, a book club at the local library or bookstore, or listen to missionaries speaking at the local church. Stretch yourself a little.

- *Find free therapy!* Strike up a conversation with the mom whose child is in therapy the same time as yours. Some parents have formed informal support groups in this way and look forward to their child's therapy time more than he does!

- *Enjoy the benefits of the Internet.* Many people use the Internet for support, which is excellent, but it's also important to get out of the house and interact with real, live people. That said, join a list group or visit a chatroom. Email is an excellent way to connect with people you know in the outside world. It's a good idea to limit the amount of time you are involved in this activity, however; it's easy to let the hours slip by while surfing the net or emailing, and it's not as satisfying as getting together with

friends. It's kind of like snack food – it feels good at the time, but then you're left feeling dissatisfied and wishing you'd had something healthier.

If this list seems overwhelming, it is a sure sign that you haven't been taking care of yourself. You don't need to go out every day and night of the week, but if you don't take care of yourself in small ways, eventually it will cost you more – it might cost you your family.

Chapter 4

Reaching Out

Tools for Building a
Community of Support

In cultures around the world, families are strongest when the extended family is available to share responsibilities and give support. However, despite our tremendous need for support, AS families often withdraw from their community. Why? We face social challenges due to our child's behaviors in public, misunderstandings that arise when we get together with people who do not have a child like ours, and shortage of time because we are busy with appointments and meetings related to our child's disability. In addition, we are often too exhausted to make the effort it takes to seek out new relationships or even maintain old ones. Part of taking care of ourselves, our marriage and our family requires reaching out into our community despite the challenges we face.

Grandparents and Extended Family

Is your family of origin somewhat receptive and reasonably well mannered? Do they understand your child's disability and are willing to be flexible in order to meet his needs? Are they supportive of you as a parent? Then, keep them! If they also offer to help out, then you should thank your lucky stars, because you have won the Extended Family Lottery. Even if there'll always be small annoyances that drive you nuts, just overlook them because they're worth the trouble.

On the other hand, you may not be as lucky in terms of support and understanding from family members. If they are generally decent folks, but are having a hard time with the AS diagnosis, you might just need to give them a little push in the right direction.

Why Don't They Just Accept That My Child Has Asperger Syndrome?

For extended family, particularly grandparents, it is hard to believe or accept something they have never heard of. Also, there is a prevalent attitude that children are being "over-diagnosed" these days, often with made-up disorders. You might hear comments like, "There was no nonsense like that when you kids were growing up," the underlying message being that they raised you right, but you aren't doing the same great job with your child. These comments may even be made by generally compassionate persons, who are genuinely worried about how their grandchild is doing. Often the only outward sign of "something wrong" is the child's behavior, so they may make the common assumption that it is a discipline problem. When you don't take their advice, they might feel frustrated because that's all the help they have to offer. And frankly, just as it's hard for parents to accept that their child has autism, it is painful for loving grandparents to let go of the dreams they had for their grandchild. It's easier to deny there is a disorder and that it's only a discipline or parenting problem, because that means it's something that can be fixed and not a permanent condition.

How Can Grandparents and Other Family Members "Get" It?

Grandparents and extended family CAN learn to understand. How well depends on the extent to which they are willing to be flexible in their idea of the world. It's not easy for any of us to accept that things aren't as we have always assumed. We need to exercise patience while they come to grips with the new reality. They also need support through the process of acceptance.

Provide reading materials. Think short and to the point: magazine articles, handouts, material off the Internet. There is information available specific to grandparents, such as on the O.A.S.I.S., Online Asperger Syndrome Information and Support, website (www.udel.edu/bkirby/asperger/). You can also tape and share news programs that discuss autism.

Take them to doctor appointments with you. Let them hear in person what the doctor or therapist has to say. If they don't take what you say seriously, they may be more receptive to professionals because they are "experts."

Share evaluation reports and IEP documents. Let them read about the specific problems your child is having. Seeing it in black and white may be painful, but they are more likely to believe something that is written than just being told.

Invite them to spend time with you as a family. Allow them to see your child's positive behaviors as well as his negative ones. Demonstrate how you handle problems, including meltdowns. Explain what it is you are doing and, afterwards, debrief with them and allow them the opportunity to answer questions.

Share your concerns and keep an ongoing dialogue about what specific challenges your family faces with your child. Be honest about the struggles your child faces and what impact it has on you. Equally important, update them on the progress your child is making through therapy and school interventions. This creates a balanced view of reality as well as keeping optimism alive for all of you.

And finally, don't forget to share the GOOD things about your child. Teach them how to see your child as you do and to recognize that he is more than "just" his diagnosis. Glow with pride at his accomplishments, and give them plenty to brag about just like any adoring grandparent!

Getting More Support From the Extended Family

Ideally your family will hear the words Asperger Syndrome and run immediately to your aid. But realistically, especially at first, even you may not know what you need. Time will make this more clear, but in the meanwhile, keep an open dialogue.

Make it very clear that what you need most from them is emotional support. Tell them it matters a great deal to you that they are willing to listen and that you are thankful that you have them in your child's life.

Try to be patient. Try to understand their emotional reactions to the news of the diagnosis and their occasional misguided comments. If they love you and their grandchild, gently explain things to them, or just let it slide a while as they adjust and grow into understanding. This may ultimately lead to an even more supportive relationship because they feel as though you are at least listening to them.

Be careful about the way you discuss money matters. Expressing worries over the financial needs of having a child with AS might make grandparents and other family members uncomfortable, especially if they aren't in a position to help you. If you choose to discuss money, make it clear you aren't asking them to solve your problem. On the other hand, if they offer, let them help. Many grandparents wish to see their money put to good use to help their grandchild.

Help create realistic expectations. Grandparents may initially be disappointed that you don't allow them to do some things they had hoped for when they imagined themselves as grandparents, such as going on overnight fishing trips or having your child fly out alone to visit them. Instead, highlight the importance of your child's relationship with them and provide alternate activities closer to home. On the other hand, if you have a neurotypical child, sending her to visit the grandparents by herself is a wonderful treat for her and for them. It can be part of her support as well as yours.

Encourage your child to be close to his grandparents and extended family. Explain that they might not always do things the way Mom and Dad do, but that they love him very much.

Don't be afraid to ask for help. If you do know of a specific way the grandparents or other extended family members can help you, ask. They might say no, but they may also have been wondering all along what they could do to help and didn't know whether to offer. Allow them the opportunity to feel useful. And be grateful.

Dealing with Family Members Who Don't Believe There Is Such a Thing as AS

You know the type. He's the one who doesn't believe there is anything "wrong" with your child other than your bad parenting. The one who says, "All that kid needs is a good spanking." He's your brother or your uncle. It might be your mother-in-law, who never did approve of your "new-fangled" way of parenting in the first place. And whether she says it or not, you just know she thinks this is somehow *your* fault. In other words, some family members don't believe you when you say your child has Asperger Syndrome. They've never heard of it, but they've seen "spoiled brats" and when they see your child refusing to eat the green bean casserole ladled onto his plate at Thanksgiving dinner, they just know your child fits that description. No need for diagnosis!

The reality is, there will be supportive people in your life and there will be "unsupportive" people, to put it lightly. They may mutter under their breath, make ignorant comments or argue outright. You can offer up information, but some people are just not willing to take the step of changing their point of view. You can't change the view of every person you and your child come into contact with, even if they are related to you – in fact, especially if they are related to you! Sometimes the most outrageous comments are made by family members because they feel more comfortable expressing themselves in a family setting. While you can't control what people think and whatever ignorant comment someone chooses to make, you can control how you react to it. You can choose to ignore or avoid them, be in constant conflict, or only deal with things as they directly affect your child.

Sometimes people outside your family unit are thinking the same thing as your outspoken relative, but are too polite to say it. Hearing the unadulterated truth of how some people think allows you the opportunity to figure out why they are wrong and to build up, point by point, evidence to counteract this kind of thinking. And, at the same time, it reinforces your own beliefs. You'll eventually be able to clearly respond to questions because you've wisely used your loud-mouth relative as practice.

When explanation falls on deaf ears, here are some ideas – some humorous, others more serious – for handling doubters who are stuck in their own way of thinking and probably will not change.

Ignore them, but think about your response if you were to speak. This is both educational and entertaining, much better than the usual family-gathering conversation. But beware of accidentally chuckling out loud to yourself as this might bring forth another string of unwanted opinions about *you.*

Have humorous responses ready to their comments. When they say, "That kid needs a good spanking!," you could counter, "Well, it certainly didn't do you any good!" or "So do you, come here!" Make sure you smile and laugh, then they won't realize you are really serious.

Use your inside information to your advantage. Everyone hates at least one thing and avoids eating it. If family members make comments about the food, or lack thereof, on your child's plate, be sure to bring that food to the next family gathering and ladle it generously on to the grumpy person's plate.

Use the "allergic" defense. "My child is allergic to lettuce (list any green vegetable or other offending food item here). Even smelling it will make him throw up instantly." This usually frightens people sufficiently to keep the salad away from the kiddie table.

Pull them aside and express how much you appreciate their concern for your child. Ask them if they would like to spend more time with your family; perhaps they'd like to drive you to your child's next therapy appointment?

Change the subject. If you don't feel like dealing with it, say, "You know, I just really don't understand this whole Aspergery-thingy either; that's why I leave it up to the doctor! Could you please pass the mashed potatoes?" Also good for diffusion: "Maybe you're right. I'll think about what you said very carefully." Then immediately put it in the recycle bin in your mind.

If all else fails, mention the most eccentric and/or dysfunctional relative. Every family has one. Say, "Too bad they weren't able to diagnose Great Uncle So-and-So back then, he might have been a different man if he'd received treatment as a child. Thank God we found it in time!" (Caution, make sure your child is not within earshot, especially if he knows who Great Uncle So-and-So was.)

Holiday Meal Suggestions

Holidays are supposed to be Norman Rockwell picture-perfect moments: The extended family gathered 'round the heavily laden table with an enormous turkey, everyone happy and thankful. The only mischief involves children peeking through their fingers during the prayer. Okay, now back to reality! Frankly, how often is it really like that for any family, much less AS families like ours? Before we bask in cruel disappointment, with a little planning you can swing the odds in your favor to have a happy family holiday after all.

1. *Call ahead to family members whose support you want to enlist.* This includes clarifying to the host so he or she understands why/how you are planning to do certain things. For example, "We'd love to stay longer, but we are planning to leave at 7:00 p.m. because we need Johnny to stick to his regular bedtime routine." This can help avoid the last-minute, "You're going already! But he's fine! We haven't had dessert yet! See, he wants to stay."

2. *Take along a couple of food items you know your child will eat.* If he decides to try something at the party, wonderful! But if not, you're covered. And if your child is on the GFCF (gluten-free cassein-free) diet, take food even if the cook reassures you, "It's fine!" Not everyone understands what contains these ingredients, so better safe than sorry.

3. *Define expectations in advance for your child.* You can write a story, draw a picture or make a list. "We will play with cousins, sit down for dinner, grown-ups will visit for one hour, we will pick up the toys and say good-bye and drive home." Making concrete decisions ahead of time not only helps your child, it can help you think ahead about what potential problems you might encounter.

5. *Remember that it is not everyone else's responsibility to consider your child's needs.* Ideally they would want to, but practically, they probably do not even have the skills. The weight of making sure your child is okay falls on you entirely.

6. *Plan how you want to supervise/monitor your child.* If there are other kids, most other adults will probably leave them to play together in another room, only checking on them from time to time (if at all). If your child typically has difficulties in social situations with peers, it is the same even if these peers are cousins. You can choose to "see how it goes" by letting them play without

any intervention, taking the risk that it may not go well. You can have a project that the kids can do together, such as crafts or a game (although that's tricky if your child is inflexible about how others play). You can check on them frequently, unobtrusively (walk by and peek into the room every so often without signaling your child or interrupting unless things aren't going well).

7. *Give countdowns to the child to prepare him.* "We're leaving in 30 minutes. We're leaving in 15 minutes." If you lose track of time and you've stayed longer than intended, don't rush the child. He still needs the transition time. Say, "Okay, you can play for 10 more minutes, then we'll pick up the toys and leave."

8. *Prepare to leave early.* Decide to cut things short if your child looks as though he is beginning to fray around the edges. Start countdown transition early if necessary.

9. *Keep it light if your child really loses it.* You may feel some pressure that you should "lay down the law" to your child in front of family members so they can see you're a "good parent." If you feel you need to say anything, you might choose to say the following with a smile, "Holidays are so stressful. He's tired and I think we've overstayed our welcome." If your child is in total meltdown, you can retire to a quiet room with him until he calms down. If there is no way to salvage the situation, we have often chosen to leave even while our child was still upset because the sooner he is out of the situation, the sooner he will feel better. Our kids often stop crying the moment they are out the door, or in the car.

Ultimately you may choose not to do family holidays at all. Some families decide to do their own quiet holidays at home where they can control the atmosphere, menu, etc. They often find it more relaxing and enjoyable. You can still get together with your extended family for dessert, or have an after-holiday get-together when there is less pressure. You will probably get disapproval from extended family members, but it's okay to choose to do what's best for your own family regardless of what others think.

Turkey Day

This year we spent Thanksgiving with our friends Elizabeth and Dave, who have 10 (!) children, after I was inspired by her email to me. (It turns out the menu did NOT include Dr. Pepper and chocolate ants after all.)

From: Elizabeth
Subject: Thanksgiving
Date: November 20, 2004
To: Kristi Sakai

Hi Kristi,

When it comes to food I always find it helpful for my child to be "in a phase." As in, "Oh, Aunt Margaret, the turkey is lovely, but she's in a chocolate ant and Dr. Pepper phase."

How about the fad defense? "Well, Uncle Ray, wearing only flannel pants and socks with the seams on the outside is the fad right now." And, "Oh yeah, refusing to brush hair is all the rage in the fourth grade, we wouldn't want to spoil his self-esteem by making him act differently than the other kids in his class now would we?"

I like your suggestions of saying the kids have allergies, Kristi. You could get pretty far with that one. "No, Grandpa, he's not taking your chair to be rude. Please understand that he has a severe long-chain poly-carbon allergy and your chair is the only one in the house that doesn't contain them in the fabric. I would make him sit on the floor, but just think of the long-chain-poly-carbons in the shag carpet." You could even buy one of those bracelets with the red cross and use it as an allergy bracelet for whatever he is adverse to this week. "Oh, so sorry, nothing with chlorophyll can even touch his plate or he'll go into anephelactic shock. I have an epi-pen, but I'd hate to have to use it."

After years of these lovely holidays when Dave asked me what I thought I'd make for Thanksgiving dinner, I told him, "Reservations."

My idea of the perfect Thanksgiving would be to invite all the kids with Aspergers, bipolar, or whatever, and their parents. Each kid could submit his two favorite holiday foods and wouldn't have to eat other people's stuff if they didn't want to. "Okay, I'll try the Dr. Pepper, but I ain't touchin' them ants." The adults could sit around eating what they want without stressing over what the kids eat or that everybody thinks they're weird. Dinner conversation would be along the lines of, "My favorite Pokémon is Pikachu." And "Oh, did you know that the hydrogen bomb has only one electron?" or "You won't believe what I found in my belly button yesterday." Parents smile and have a glass of wine with their dessert. –Elizabeth

Creating Your Own Extended Family

Ideally we would all come from supportive families who have not only the desire to understand our child's disability, but also the resources to support us. If you are fortunate to have that, don't take it for granted. It's not the norm.

Most families who are faced with the enormous challenges of caring for a child with a disability do not have family support. Their families may live far away, their own circumstances may limit their ability to be involved or they may choose not to be involved for a variety of reasons. Some parents choose not to include their family of origin in their daily lives because they do not offer a healthy place to find emotional support. This can be true of any family, whether or not you have a child with autism. As a result, you may feel overwhelmed, alone, adrift without anyone to fall back on. All is not lost; there is support out there! So where on earth do we start?

No Way! There Can't Possibly Be People Out There Like Us!

While your family might *seem* unusual, you might discover there are more of us out there than you realize. We're like a (not-so) secret society, and if you know the secret handshake, then you're in! (Trust me, you DO.) Many families find their strongest connections with other Asperger Families because who can better understand their needs? Where do you find folks like us?

Look in the obvious places. You can start by turning to support groups, informational meetings, conferences and even waiting rooms to meet other parents.

Sometimes totally unexpected places hold great treasures. Don't turn your nose up at friends of friends. It's called "networking," and it works in this context, too. And don't forget to keep your eyes peeled in non-autism-related activities. I've been shoe shopping, dropped the word "autism" and folks came running to talk. (By the way, if the very nice man whose grandson has AS is reading this: I love the boots!)

***Put on your Asperger-colored glasses once
more!*** As you become more aware of your
child's issues, you'll have new eyes with
which to view the world. You'll begin to recognize autistic behavior all around you. It
might be an adult who has sensory issues
like your child, or it might be a frazzled parent at the grocery store whose child is
going berserk in an all-too familiar way.
Suddenly you realize there are many families
like yours, maybe right in your neighborhood.

Developing the Relationship

Relationships with other families like yours
won't be conventional, to say the least.
And like all things worthwhile, it'll take planning
and effort. Despite the difficulties involved, it is important to take
the time and energy to make and maintain those connections.
Every relationship has negotiations, and considerations, only our
families have a few more.

Do we get the crowd together? Sometimes you will. You'll be able
to plan parties and events with your children's needs in mind.
Ground rules can be laid beforehand, such as the length of time
and how leaving will be handled – all with the mutual knowledge
that things may need to be cut short. Some families have the special kind of relationship where they can say directly, "My son isn't
doing well. I'm sorry but it's time for you to go" – again with the
understanding that the other family may need an adjustment period
for their own child at this change of plans. These kinds of gatherings can be chaotic, but there is a certain security in knowing your
family is welcome and accepted just as it is. There is a sense of
safety in knowing friends like these.

What if getting together is too stressful? Often schedules or children's conflicting needs preclude actually getting the gang together,
but this doesn't eliminate potential friendship. Many a friendship is
primarily forged and maintained by phone and email. The good news
about this is that both parties understand the challenges you face in

communicating with the kids underfoot. You can also plan outings that do not include the kids, which is a break for both of you.

Will we babysit each other's kids? Perhaps. Asperger Parents who have similar parenting styles may find trading off the kids works out marvelously. Or maybe you are both overwhelmed and cannot handle the additional load even if it is reciprocated. It may also depend on the ages of the children and their developmental level. Remember, what is not possible now might eventually work out; give it time.

Nothing reinforces good parenting of any kind more than people who share your values. Friends who understand our children's needs are priceless, and irreplaceable once you find them. They will become more than your community of support, they will become your extended family.

What About Our Child's Relationships?

There is a pervasive belief that people with autism spectrum disorders do not desire or require connecting with others. Is this true or false? It depends on the person, his age, his life experiences that led to isolation by choice or design and a multitude of other factors. All human beings benefit from caring connections, even if their own response seem limited. We have seen children who started out as quiet loners who weren't interested in others grow to value their relationships with peers perhaps even more than neurotypicals.

Reconnecting

One place to look for support is the community you were involved with before your child was diagnosed. These connections may be strained because of the difficulties you've encountered. For example, your family may not have been able to attend church recently because your child hasn't been doing well. Or perhaps you've withdrawn because you've felt too overwhelmed. It's important to try to re-establish these connections if possible. Not everyone will be a candidate for renewed friendship; it's a given that some people will not understand. But don't assume you won't be accepted. Most people who truly care about you will *try* to understand.

A True Friend

- *Learns how to cook a GFCF meal for your family and drops it by when you are at the end of your rope.*

- *Knows something's up when she calls just from the way you say, "hello?"*

- *Listens to you lament about your son's school for the 1,000th time.*

- *Knows you well enough to tell you on occasion to shut up and get over it.*

- *Attends IEP meetings with you and continues to debate on your child's behalf even though you have left the table to go cry in the ladies room.*

- *Tolerates phone conversations that go like this, "Just a second, 'GET OFF YOUR BROTHER'S HEAD RIGHT NOW!' So, what was it you were saying?"*

- *Answers truthfully when you ask her, "Does this make me look fat?" and tells you which jeans make your fanny look smaller.*

- *Will talk you into dying your hair a new color she thinks is "perfect" for you, and then laugh with you and agree it looks awful.*

- *Meets you when you have an "emergency" such as you think you will die if you don't get out of the house and talk to another adult.*

- *Meets you in a real emergency, like when your child is taken to the hospital, and remembers to call your other friends to encourage them to also give you support. Plus, brings you something to eat because you aren't thinking about yourself, but she is.*

- *Laughs at the ridiculous emails you send her at 3:00 a.m. that make absolutely no sense, and then says you are hilarious and that you should write a book.*

- *Has cried the same tears over her child as you have over yours, so she knows you like no one else can because both of your hearts have been broken and healed in the same way.*

Handling Heartfelt Offers of Help

Even when people are kind enough to offer help, many parents are either concerned about burdening others or take such offers as criticism of their ability to manage on their own, and therefore decline. It is easy to fall into the trap of thinking all comments, questions and offers are critical judgment about your parenting. While that may be true in some cases, how can we find the connections with people we need without initially giving them the benefit of the doubt? Many people, including ourselves, feel a great sense of satisfaction in helping others. There is no shame in accepting something that is freely given with sincere intentions.

Remember the learning curve. It's true, others may not truly understand your child's limitations or behavior at first, but if they are genuinely trying to minister to your family, they will be willing to listen and learn. You don't have to take them up on their offer to drop your child off for the entire day without any clue of what they are in for, because that would probably be (a) too stressful for your child or (b) the last time they would offer! But you can let them entertain your child for a while at an event while you grab something to eat, or help your child with an activity while you are there, keeping an eye from a distance in case you need to intervene and model how to handle your child's needs. These small things can make your life easier because they build on each other. Eventually you will discover whether they are equipped with the skills necessary to watch your child for longer periods of time.

Ask and you shall receive. Often folks want to offer support and comfort, but don't know what you need. As difficult as it is to ask, expressing your needs directly is often a relief to those who are seeking to help. For example, feeling nervous about attending an important medical appointment or evaluation by yourself with your child? How about asking them to go along with you? They can take your child for a walk in the hall if you need to speak to the professional alone, and later they can help you decompress as you drive home together. You may not be able to give them the identical support in return, but your friendship is just as valuable in other ways.

Express your emotional needs. Tell your friends when you are asking for advice, and when what you really need is just for them to listen and not try to "fix" anything. A phone call when you are upset to a person who has been sympathetic can recharge your batteries and give you more faith in making those connections. Although it may appear that you are the needier one because you have your hands full, it makes some people feel good about themselves to offer support. Plus, sometimes you'll be able to reciprocate.

Know you're not the only one. Don't think you've cornered the market on suffering and that no one will understand you or your family. Everyone has something in their life that is challenging; you can be friends with someone who isn't in your identical situation. If they want to be your friend, they'll want to understand, just as you'll want to understand their lives. Sharing the different challenges we face in life is what creates those connections.

Attending Community Events

Being part of a community is important, but attending social events is often challenging for families who have a child with an autism spectrum disorder. However, that doesn't mean that you are doomed to never leave the house. Don't forget the tools discussed in Chapter 2, priming, predicting, countdown, reward and wrap-up, and keep the event short to increase the odds of success. Here are a few other suggestions that have worked well for many Asperger Families.

Choose events your AS child enjoys. This seems obvious, but we've dragged our kids to "grown-up" things and all of us would have been happier if we'd gotten a babysitter. If the event is something your child is particularly interested in, his motivation is higher and he may be more cooperative. But even if he is enjoying himself, remember: *keep it short to ensure success*. My grandpa used to say, "The time to leave is when everybody is still having a good time." Good advice!

Remember that some days are better than others. Our kids fluctuate and are more capable one day than another. If he's not having a "good" day, adding to his stress load with more expectations probably isn't going to help the situation. It's disappointing to cancel fun plans, but better to wait for a "good" day to make those happy family memories.

Take two cars. Half the family goes home before anyone gets too overwhelmed, the other half can stay if they aren't ready to go. This is particularly important if the NT sibling is having a good time and doesn't want to leave.

"Divide and conquer." One parent stays home with the AS child who might not really want to attend the event, the other goes out alone or with the other children. No partner? This is an excellent use of respite care, as discussed in the following pages.

If people question why you are separating your family this way, take this opportunity to be open about the challenges your child has in public. If they have witnessed his behavior, they may already be more aware than you realize about how hard it is for you. Their questions mean they are reaching out to you; let them.

Respite

It is increasingly rare for extended families to share in the day-to-day joys and burdens of raising children. Many parents rely on childcare, both during the day when they work and at other times when they have to attend meetings, go to appointments or take some time for themselves. But what about families with special needs? Who is willing and, even more important, able to properly care for your child?

Perhaps you've tried respite care and experienced "dismal failures" because your child was in distress when you left him because his needs weren't properly met. Although there may be times when your child (any child) will be unhappy when left by his parents, it is important to remember that this happens even in your own care! It doesn't have to be a traumatic experience for your child to be left in somebody else's care and a guilt-inducing experience for you. You can find good respite care. Your child can be well taken care of and even be happy in your absence. It takes time and motivation to find the right place/person, something I know you've already practiced!

Who Are You Looking For?

A respite provider isn't a "babysitter." He or she is part of your community of support. You do not have to have someone who specializes in caring for children with special needs or AS. It is more important that the person is gentle, understanding and willing to learn the skills necessary to care for your child. Such a person must be open to ideas that sometimes run contrary to standard discipline techniques.

When looking for the right person, ask such questions as:

- Do they express an interest in learning new things?

- Are they willing to read about AS? It doesn't necessarily have to be a book; it can be short explanations off the Internet, DVDs, etc.

- Are they willing to be flexible and abide by your plans?

Important Uses for Respite

Think outside the box. Respite isn't just for date night (although that's appealing too!). Having a support person for your family creates new opportunities for living a more balanced life. Here are some purposes for which a support person might come in handy:

- *To stay with your neurotypical child when you take your AS child to the doctor or therapy so s/he doesn't have to sit in the waiting room – again.*

- *To stay with your AS child so you can take your neurotypical child out to do an activity of her choice – movie, eat out, video arcade, mall, community event – and other places that your AS child may not enjoy.*

- *To stay with all your children so you can go out with your spouse.*

- *To watch the children in an emergency.*

- *To go along on a family activity, such as the community pool, to be extra eyes and hands.*

- *To serve as a trusted adult to teach your child he can depend on others besides you.*

- *To play with your kids while you catch up on the laundry, or any of the other seemingly endless household tasks.*

- *To pick up and transport children from school, or to therapy.*

- *To receive the children when they get off the bus if there is a gap in travel time because you have another appointment elsewhere.*

You may find that your respite providers are not only excellent resources for watching your kids, they may also have some insights about behaviors they see when they are with your child and/or develop their own strategies to help. It is greatly reassuring at times to have somebody to bounce ideas off of. Such a person may not be a parent, but may grow to care about you and your family and become an important support for you as well as your child. This person may very well become an extended family member your children look forward to seeing.

Where Do You Find Respite?

Sometimes a respite provider may be found by pure coincidence. More often, however, a more careful search is necessary.

Word of mouth from other AS families. If your friends are already receiving excellent care from a respite provider, you may decide to "share." The upside to this arrangement is that you know the provider is flexible and understanding of your child's special needs. The downside is that you may occasionally run into scheduling conflicts because you both need respite at the same time. If you know the respite provider has the skills and is willing, you might even arrange for her to watch both of the children at the same time. Some families who get together hire a shared respite provider to be at a mutual gathering so they can relax a little.

Disability services organizations. Organizations and agencies such as Developmental Disability, ARC and other community support services sometimes offer respite services. The eligibility criteria vary, so even if your family does not qualify for one, keep checking. Some of the determination factors include IQ, assessments, specific disability or income level.

Graduate students. Many families have found that graduate students with majors in special education or psychology make excellent respite providers. Their motivation is usually strong to meet the child's needs, and this is an excellent opportunity for the students to learn first-hand the needs of the type of families they will eventually work with. Some programs even give these students credit for spending time with AS and other special needs families.

Close friends' adult children. Such people can be especially help-ful if they were raised with a special needs sibling. They sometimes have insight even you do not have.

Playing It Safe

Regardless of where you find respite providers, it is important to remember that they are strangers in your home, even if they are acquaintances. It should go without saying that you take all precau-tions to protect your child. Don't let embarrassment override your good sense. Just do it.

Check references. Many parents do not think of themselves as employers, and therefore do not go through a real interview process, which includes checking with past employers. Your respite provider should be happy to provide you with this kind of informa-tion; if not, beware.

Conduct background checks. Even if you found your respite provider through a service organization, do not assume a back-ground check has been performed. Ask, and if you are not satis-fied, do it yourself; it's easy. Go online, type "background check" into the search engine and soon will pop up an endless list of agen-cies that do this. If you don't have the provider's social security number (which you must have if you are going to deduct childcare from your taxes), a full name and date of birth (year) are sufficient for most purposes.

Preparation and Training

Give your child and yourself time to feel comfortable with the new person. Model and train, and observe the provider interact with your child. The first several times you may simply have the respite provider come to the house and hang out with your child while you catch up on the house, cook, or do a project. In fact, many parents do this on an ongoing basis even after the respite provider is trained because it gives the child one-on-one attention and frees them up for other at home projects. At first you will probably have many interruptions; you might have to stop what you are doing, step in and model how to care for your child's needs. Don't give up; the time you spend doing this will pay off over the long haul for both you and your child.

People You Probably Do Not Want As Your Respite Provider

- *Just because someone offers to doesn't mean you should let them. You might consider this as an act of revenge on a clueless relative, but unfortunately it might be too distressing to your child.*

- *Any know-it-all who says smugly, "Give me a weekend with him and I'll straighten him out!" (Although the temptation might be to say, "What are you doing THIS weekend? I'd like to go out of town!")*

- *Your brother, who says, "There ain't nothin' wrong with that boy; he just needs a good spanking."*

- *Your aunt who has a "Clean Your Plate" policy at her house.*

- *The lady at church who thinks Pokémon or Yu-gi-oh are evil tools of the devil – ditto for anyone who burns Harry Potter books.*

- *Your fifth-grade teacher, who said, "If I had my own children, I'd drown them!" (True story!)*

Good Choice:
The lady who sees your child throw himself on the floor sobbing and says, "Poor baby, he's having a rough day."

Bad Choice:
The lady who sees your child throw himself on the floor and says, "Only babies do that!"

Professionals

Some of your most significant relationships will not be confined to your immediate circle of friends. As an Asperger Parent you will come into contact with a mix of professionals who are part of your child's life, and therefore yours as well. They are a crucial part of your community of support.

Building a Solid Base of Support

It is important to build a solid relationship with the professionals who work with your children, such as therapists, doctors and school staff. Why?

It's a matter of trust. You are entrusting your child's care into these people's hands, so you must be able to trust their judgment and expertise. It goes beyond credentials; it is the sense of knowing the person has your child's best interests at heart. Building trust involves getting a sense of who the person is, and where his or her priorities lie. It is important to understand this because sometimes things go "wrong" and all you might have to guide you at that moment is the trust you have built in that relationship.

They need to trust you, too. It's a two-way street. A parent's competence is a factor in making decisions about the child's treatment. Professionals come into contact with a wide variety of parents, many of whom are *not* plugged-in, capable parents. Actively involved, attentive parents gain respect and, ultimately, trust.

How does this benefit your family? For one, the professional will believe you if there is something out of the box going on with your child, or an unusual situation occurs (and with our kids it's often the case). They know you and will take your word for it. This saves frustration and time for both of you. They will also trust that you are following through on their treatment and that the reason why something isn't working has nothing to do with some shortcoming on your part.

Human nature dictates. It's easier to work with people you have a mutual affinity for, or at the very least, respect for. Professionals may have to serve many people they do not even like, but as human beings they prefer to work with those they like. This edge of acceptance from the professional and vice versa helps us all feel like a team and encourages us to work hard together.

We're in it for the long haul. Our children have a life-long disorder that isn't going away. We need to build a strong and connected team that will last for many years. While it's true that you will jetti-son some ineffective team members from time to time, eventually, if you have a good working relationship you'll have people who will stick with you.

Tools for Building the Support Team

To create relationships with professionals, like all others, takes effort. But it also pays off in the long run because you have many years of raising your AS child. A healthy relationship with his team of professionals makes the road easier. Here are a few things to keep in mind.

Treat them with respect. This is simple logic, but you'd be sur-prised how often parents do not see their child's professional provider as deserving of respect. In order to receive respect our-selves, we must give it. This isn't about blind acceptance of what they have to say, nor is it offering your child up on the altar of medi-cine in pure worship and awe of the doctor. It is about remembering that they have dedicated their lives to helping children like ours. Speak and listen respectfully and value their time. Say "thank you." Just because it's their job doesn't mean they don't deserve recogni-tion for it. Plenty of people do their jobs, but not well. Recognize the people who DO.

Learn as much as you can from them. Most professionals do not resent questions. Parents who ask questions are the ones who are plugged in. The more you understand, the better you can work as a team for the benefit of your child. You will garner more respect if you listen. Consider what they have to say carefully and do additional research.

Remember they are human beings, too. We often forget that professionals are people just like us. They make mistakes, experience bad days and have emotions involved in their job. That is reality. As long as it doesn't negatively impact your child's treatment over the long run, be a little forgiving of that. In all likelihood, when it's your turn to have an "off" day, they'll be patient with you.

Think of them. This is a variation on the above, but it's a little more personal. In remembering they are human beings, think of what makes people feel good about themselves. It can be simple things like remembering to write them a thank-you when you've gone through a crisis with your child and they were there for your family. It can be more elaborate such as secretly finding out when their birthday is and doing something extra special for them on that day. It can even be something as small as picking a flower from your garden and having your child give it to them at his appointment.

What If There Is Conflict?

There are times of conflict and disagreement in most relationships. Professional ones are no different, particularly when you are dealing with matters related to your child and your emotions naturally run high because so much is at stake. How do we handle conflict in a professional relationship?

Approach them with an attitude of respect. Again, professionals are valued members of your community of support. If you fly off the handle, you may very well lose this relationship and it might be a bridge you regret burning. If you have concerns and approach them with a respectful attitude, state your perceptions and are willing to listen, not only will you be able to salvage the relationship, you may create a healthier, stronger one.

Write out your concerns. Afraid you'll lose your temper? Write your concerns down before speaking. Or write an email or letter. Be careful of the tone, just as you would the tone of your voice.

Ask them to help you problem solve. If you run into a situation where you are concerned about how something is handled, ask the appropriate professional to help you fix it. Simply bringing it to the professional's attention might be all that is required because he already has a solution in mind.

Lose control of your emotions? Apologize. It's all right to have strong emotions when it comes to the treatment and care of your child. From time to time we might cry. That's okay. In some cases, we might even raise our voices. That is *not* okay. They may recognize what is happening and be forgiving, but they shouldn't have to. If you are crossing the line, you know it. Even if you're not wrong about what you're saying, apologize for the attitude.

Remember, they are TRYING. In discussing this subject recently with our doctor, she said the most important thing she wished parents understood is, "We care about these kids, and we are trying our best." They may not always be "right" about everything. Sometimes medicine is part science and part art, so there are variables that must be constantly considered, and educated, but quick, judgment calls to be made. Every child is different; no one responds the same way to treatment, and things sometimes go "wrong." This isn't the professionals' fault. They are in there fighting the good fight on behalf of our kids. Whenever possible we should fight *with* them and not against them.

Part ways as amicably as possible. There are times when you must remove your child from someone's care for any variety of reasons. If someone has dropped the ball, you should let them know what your concerns are, and if they fail to correct the situation to the best of their ability, terminate the relationship. But try not to burn bridges, for several reasons. One, you don't know how they are connected to other members of your support team. They may have a working relationship with the provider you choose to replace them. It doesn't bode well to start out on a bad foot with the next guy. And don't complain to your new provider about the incompetence of the last guy. This is a red flag that will keep his or her guard up. And, in a worst-case scenario, if your replacement provider falls through, you may need the former guy in a pinch. You don't want to be left hanging because you shot your mouth off as you stomped out the door.

What Does This Teach Our Child?

Building a relationship with the professionals in your child's life teaches him many important lessons, such as awareness of the needs of others, social skills and good manners, not to mention being appreciative of those who help you.

Children who have disabilities often build strong bonds with the adults who care for them, but there is a down-side. What can happen is that because they spend so much time in therapy and seeing various doctors, their sole significant relationships outside of their immediate family are professionals. From time to time these relationships may have to end. A doctor may retire, a special education teacher moves to another district. While this is an important life lesson for our children, it can be very painful for them. They may not be able to understand why Dr. So-and-So is no longer their "friend."

So what can be done about this dilemma? Make sure that your child has a broad and varied community of support that includes friends, family and professionals so when one drops out, there is another to continue the support. Remember, some day, even YOU will no longer be here for him. So make sure other people are. Don't leave your child without a net.

As you work on having open communication and building trust with your child's team, you may find that you not only create a good working relationship with these professionals, but that you become attached to them as well. There is something significant about the people in your child's life who care about him, who listen to *your* concerns and meet *his* needs. We start to care about them and to depend on their good judgment. This helps us feel more supported as parents and gives us added strength to get through difficult times. 🔨

Chapter 5

A Marriage of Inconvenience

Tools for Building a Relationship with the School

Some of the most significant people in your child's life are the school staff: the classroom, speech and special education teachers, as well as educational assistants and others he sees on a daily basis. But there are other people, such as school administrators, who may not even know your child, much less have ongoing contact with him. And yet, these people have a great deal of power to make decisions regarding his immediate and consequently his long-term future. You, on the other hand, as a plugged-in parent, will have many interactions with this mixed bag of school professionals. It can be intimidating to face this panel of people who are seemingly of one mind about what your child's needs are. How on earth do you get them to listen to you when you don't agree?

This chapter offers some insights on building these relationships and a few suggestions to tip the scales a little more in favor of academic success for your child.

Tied by the Bonds of Education

Sometimes the relationship you have with school staff is sort of like being in an arranged marriage for the sake of the children. A marriage of seemingly ill-conceived INconvenience. You might not even like each other. If you lined up a thousand people as potential relationship partners, they wouldn't make it through the first rose ceremony. But set aside your romantic notions of free choice, in this case you've arrived for the wedding buying a pig in a poke, and you're tied by the bonds of education for the duration. Despite the hardship of this mismatched pairing, if you want to tilt the odds in your child's favor of potential academic success, you have to learn to play nice. After all, we're stuck with these people until our child leaves their school (or until either of us has a nervous breakdown).

You smile, as you press for what you want. Tempers flare occasionally, but you keep it outside of the child's hearing range. As in most relationships, it works better if there's frequent communication, so you work on it. You might discover they have some attributes that complement your own. You might even find that you develop a reasonable working relationship with your strange bedfellows, despite yourself. And the longer you work with them, the more clearly you learn to see their perspective. If you're lucky, it will be mutual.

Okay, so there will always be hopeless dinosaurs, and you just do the best you can with them and breathe a sigh of relief when they become extinct, er, I mean RETIRE. But once in a while you might find yourself surprised that the staff member you butt heads with the most isn't the enemy after all. I often tell my children, "Do it until you feel it." This means, you might not feel like doing something, or treating someone a certain way, but you'll develop the habit. Here's the thing about inescapable relationships. Over time as you keep up the pretense of respecting these people, it might turn out that you actually DO.

Tools for Communication

It is important to develop a relationship with the school staff. As with other professionals, communication is key. School staff carry a heavy burden of many children with various needs and in most cases welcome actively involved parents. However, some parents of children in special ed. garner a "special" reputation. This is partly the nature of SPED because there are constant issues that require us to call or show up at the school. And when things go wrong, we aren't always in the best frame of mind! This can lead to an adversarial relationship with the staff, which is counterproductive in most cases.

It is important to speak up when things are not going well, and to make sure our children are well taken care of. But if this is our only contact with the staff, they will be increasingly reluctant to communicate with us. What are some ways to improve this? We need to take the initiative by discussing ways to implement communication tools.

Daily Schedule

This involves the child having a picture or written schedule for each class period with space to write in a brief comment about what happened throughout the day. Before the child leaves for the day, staff makes a copy and sends it home to the parents. Not only is this information helpful for tracking your child's progress throughout the day, it can be used as an important conversational tool with your child. Instead of saying, "How was your day?" and getting the usual one-word answer, "Fine," you can say, "I see you studied the Egyptians in social studies today! Did you learn about mummies?" The child's response is likely to be more enthusiastic. And, if your child has behavior issues consistently during a specific activity or time of day, the schedule can easily convey the pattern for both staff and parents.

Communication Notebook

Many schools have instituted a system whereby a notebook goes back and forth between home and school. This is a good way for the staff to relate the things that are working, or not working well, for your child. This free exchange and ongoing dialogue allows for the ability to almost instantly adjust and make changes. It also gives you added insight into what might be triggering your child. Finally, it allows you the opportunity to make positive comments and suggestions. In brief, it allows you to work with each other as a closer-knit team.

Daily Schedule

Date:
Student:

		Good	Great	Notes
8:15-9:00 Reading				
9:00-9:45 Math				
9:45-10:20 Spelling				
10:20-10:40 Recess				
10:40-11:00 Reward				
11:00-11:30 P.E.				
11:30-12:00 Speech				
12:00-12:40 Lunch				
12:40-1:10 Science				
1:20-2:10 Social Studies				
2:10-2:30 Recess				
2:30-3:00 Art				

Dear Mrs. Smith,

Today Sean had trouble at recess; he was crying and would not tell us what had happened. After that he refused to cooperate in any of his afternoon activities. Also, his class is going on a field trip on Thursday, please sign the permission slip if you want him to go.

Mrs. Jones

The parent's reply in the notebook, which is sent back to the school:

Dear Mrs. Jones,

I asked Sean what happened on the playground. He said that he wanted to play ball but the other children wouldn't let him participate. Could the playground monitor please keep an eye on this? Maybe we need to problem solve about this if it continues to be a problem. Sean does not want to go on the field trip with his class. Can he stay in the resource room that day?

Mrs. Smith

Mrs. Smith,

Sean cannot stay in the resource room on Thursday because there is no staff available. Another option is for him to stay with the art teacher and make crafts while his class is gone. I talked with the playground monitor and she said Sean played alone again today. He isn't the only child having trouble on the playground. We're thinking about having some organized activities during lunch recess that Sean and some other kids might be interested in. Maybe an outside chess group?

Mrs. Jones.

Through such communication school staff and parents are able to quickly problem solve, share ideas and come up with solutions. Also, any intensity of feelings is diffused because there is the expectation of ongoing communication instead of only communicating when there is a problem.

Email

Although many schools are not allowed to use the child's name in Internet communication due to confidentiality, they can use initials. 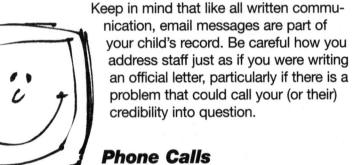 Keep in mind that like all written communication, email messages are part of your child's record. Be careful how you address staff just as if you were writing an official letter, particularly if there is a problem that could call your (or their) credibility into question.

Phone Calls

If your child was having a rough morning and got on the bus in a particularly agitated state, a quick call to the classroom or resource teacher to tip her off is usually appreciated. This allows her to prepare, for example, by having a staff member meet the child directly from the bus and escort him to home base or another place where he can relax before entering the classroom.

On the Sly

Look for opportunities to communicate with staff members unofficially and listen carefully. This includes a quick update from the assistant or teacher when you pick up your child, a comment to or from the bus driver or the office secretary. These people know more than you realize and have valuable insights about how you can help your child be more successful at school. Do not use this information "officially," however, if your school frowns on this type of communication.

It is also important to know if and when to speak to staff. Do not pull staff aside during school hours to pester, grill or, worst of all, give them a verbal thrashing. How would you like it if your son's teacher showed up at your job and chewed you out in front of your coworkers or clients?

School hours are not the time or place to confront staff. Save your negative observations for if and when they are appropriate. And even with those, weigh the importance of them. As with anything else, pick your battles, don't nitpick over the obscure and relatively unimportant. Finally, when you drop by the school, it is a wonderful opportunity to look for things that they are doing right and to make positive comments about them. Maybe they will be less likely to cringe at the sight of you entering the school!

Meetings

Perhaps one of the most difficult experiences for parents is school meetings, whether it's a parent-teacher conference or the dreaded IEP meeting. It is overwhelming to walk into a school where you are directed to sit in a chair that is just the right size ... if you are a first grader ... and in that uncomfortable state, listen to the professionals tell you what's "wrong" with your child. This can be intimidating because you may think of yourself as "only" a parent, or you may feel as though you are being treated as a child yourself.

This isn't usually intentional. These are teachers, after all, and even as grownups it's easy to fall under the intimidating spell that transports you back to elementary school. Add to that having to hear about behavior issues, and other not-so-pleasant news about your child, and it can be an excruciating experience. But with the proper preparation you can override the intimidation factor and walk in with self-assurance. Because: You are the expert on your child above anyone else. You have a component to offer the IEP team that is crucial, and it is your job to share the benefit of your wisdom with them. Here are some keys to having a more successful meeting experience.

Put your feelers out. Before meetings try to feel out issues that might come up by, for example, having regular and ongoing contact with the school staff, as suggested above, and listening to what their concerns are.

Find secret allies. Find supporters among the school staff. These are people who may or may not overtly show they are backing you during a meeting, but who often give you inside information that is very helpful and let you be the bad guy who pushes for services for the child. Maybe it's the teacher who knows the other staff member doesn't quite "get" it and gives you the heads-up on how to approach various people in order to get them to listen.

Take the chip off your shoulder. Walk in with an open mind about the staff, even if you've had conflict in the past. Some of the things you've done in between may have mended your working relationship. Be prepared, but remember, if you are already keyed up for a fight, it might become a self-fulfilled prophecy.

Listen. This is extremely important. Many parents walk in so sure of themselves that they come on too strong. The staff is much more likely to respond to your opinions/ideas if you are willing to first listen to what they have to say and consider it carefully.

Take charge. Nevertheless, sometimes you do need to "take charge" of the meeting from the outset. These are times when there has been a great deal of conflict before the meeting, which is why you are there. Walk in with back-up support. I have taken as many as four people to an IEP meeting, including two occupational therapists, a DD caseworker and a friend. At times I have made up my agenda ahead of time and handed it out at the meeting. In these circumstances, take the initiative to speak first and introduce the team members as each staff member enters the room. This puts you in the driver's seat.

What If Things Get Heated?

Meetings do not always go smoothly. We may get upset when we are in disagreement about something we feel strongly about, perhaps even *seemingly* out of proportion to the issue at hand. This is because, once again, we are not just thinking about the short-term consequences of our child not receiving a certain support or service, we are thinking about the long-term investment in his future. When you need to keep your wits about you, keep the following in mind.

Keep your goals in focus. What are the true short-term and long-term goals you have in mind for your child? Use this information to explain to staff the importance of the service or support your child needs to receive.

Check yourself. Are you being reasonable? Are you asking for something that the school realistically cannot give you, or simply will not? It's important to differentiate between the two.

Prioritize. Bottom line, what are you willing to give up and what are you willing to fight to the death over? Give in a little on the "nice to haves" and stick to your guns on the "must haves."

Handle yourself with dignity. If the school staff is being unreasonable, argumentative or is talking down to you, take charge. Be assertive. But if you are angry, never resort to personal attacks. There is a difference between being emotional and being passionate, although it can be a fine line. Allow them to speak, but not to browbeat you. This is another reason why having an advocate with you is important; she can act as a witness and take notes, as well as rein you in if necessary. If you get too hot under the collar, let your advocate step in for you.

Leave if you need to. You can also discontinue the meeting and reschedule when cooler heads prevail.

Gone a little over the top? In our passionate zest for conveying the importance of a significant issue, we might (I say "we" as in "I") go a little too far and cross over into the land of angry irrational parent. It's true, sometimes we do! At times we do need to flex our parenting muscles and show we're not going to be bullied, but we also need to realize when we're using a sledge hammer and it isn't really necessary. Nothing lost on an apology, whether it's in the middle of the meeting or later.

Queen Bee

IEP, to the uninitiated, stands for individualized education program. In theory, the purpose of an IEP meeting and related documents is to set up a program that is appropriate for a child in special educa-

tion, including educational goals and services provided by the district. In reality, what often happens is that you sit for an hour listening to everything that is wrong with your child, how terribly he is doing in school and what services the district will not be providing to help. It's preferable to attend the meeting with "muscle," a.k.a. an advocate who has a long, impressive title even if all she does is sit quietly and look official.

I remember well the spring of my first IEP meeting. The staff was warm and friendly, enthusiastic and flexible. They not only welcomed my ideas, they applauded them. We signed the IEP with beaming smiles, all parties perfectly satisfied that we had a well-thought-out and appropriate plan for my son. A blissful summer passed as we anticipated the next school year with blind optimism. But a surprise was waiting in the fall, which transformed me from the virgin IEP bride to the jaded mother I am today. The staff on our IEP team had failed to mention that they were all leaving within days of our meeting for greener district pastures. That is, they made lame-duck proclamations in the spring with fingers crossed, not knowing who would fill their shoes in the fall.

Rapid staff turnover means that parents spend a great deal of time explaining their children's special needs and how to meet them, but the most significant roadblock is commonly the fixed notions staff have about who special ed. parents are. By the end of the year we've built relationships and most folks are on board with us. They've learned that when we say something works best for our child, we are usually right. Trust is developed. But why waste an entire year?

As a hobby beekeeper I must occasionally re-queen a hive. The queen arrives inside a tiny cage that has a removable cork in one end. I pull out the cork and insert a gummy bear into the opening. When I place the cage inside the hive, the colony immediately clusters around the queen cage, but it's not the warm homecoming she is expecting. As far as they know, she isn't their queen. If they had immediate access to her, they'd kill her instantly. However, by the time they nibble their way through the gummy bear, they've gotten used to her scent and she emerges as The Queen. They not only accept her – they are willing to die for her.

On a queening day I had an "Ah ha" moment. What I really need for *the next IEP meeting is a Queen cage of my own. Every year we have a new colony of workers, people who don't know me and aren't clued into the fact that I'm actually **their** Queen. I can see it now: I arrive carried on a litter, my Queen cage protecting me from the stings of the school staff, an enticing giant gummy bear glistening from the portal. They may fully intend to slay me with their barbs, but by the time they've nibbled their way to me they'll have gotten used to my scent and recognize me forever after as The Queen Bee of the IEP.*

What If You Cry?

This isn't a business meeting, and although these are professionals and you'd like to behave professionally too, first and foremost you are a parent. Consequently, you are affected by emotions when they are talking about your child. It's all right to cry. But if you are worried that you might and you don't want to, here are a few tips for how to avoid it.

1. *Be prepared.* The more prepared you are to explain your position, and the more supported you are in it, the less likely you are to be caught off guard and become overly emotional.

2. *Do some deep breathing.* When you are caught off guard and feel as though you are going to cry, breathe deeply from your stomach. Try not to look at the people who are upsetting you. This is also a good time for your advocate to step in and speak for you.

3. *Leave the room.* You don't have to make an explanation, just say, "Excuse me for a minute," and go to the ladies room. You can leave your advocate in the room to continue handling things, or if you feel you need support, you can motion for her to follow you. However, you're more likely to cry if you have someone sympathetic with you. Take as much time as you need; don't worry about everyone waiting. The meeting can be re-scheduled, if necessary.

4. *Examine the reasons for your upset.* If you find you are crying frequently in meetings, it might be that you are extremely frustrated with the school for good reason. A second possibility is

that there is more going on than just the meeting. Crying, frustration and anger are often symptoms of related issues.

- Perhaps you are feeling powerless because no one is listening to what your child needs. Or maybe you feel inadequate in the professional setting. Remind yourself that you know your child best. Your job is just as important as theirs.

- Maybe you are still grieving over your child's diagnosis and the challenges your family is facing. Hearing all the things that are going "wrong" at school brings up those feelings and along with them sometimes, tears. This doesn't mean that you are imagining the problems at school, or that you are overreacting. It does mean that you need extra support from your community.

- Being sad, angry and overwhelmed can also be signs that you aren't taking good care of yourself. You are carrying a heavy load, and maybe you need a little break before a big meeting so you'll walk in more relaxed and confident.

5. *Cry ahead of time.* Some parents, particularly moms, have found that they are easy criers at meetings. Nothing wrong with that, but if this is you and you find it interferes with your ability to communicate, try to cry it out ahead of time. The night before, maybe have an emotional conversation with your friend or spouse, read painful evaluations and think of worst-case scenarios to trigger the tears. Cry it out and walk in with a dry well. It sounds weird, but it works!

6. *And for heaven's sake, don't forget to wear waterproof mascara!* Just in case.

Advocates

As mentioned, it is advisable to take an advocate with you to IEP and other important school meetings. An advocate is someone who offers you both physical and emotional support, and who hopefully also offers complementary skills.

Who Can Be an Advocate?

Anyone of your choosing can be an advocate, preferably in this order.

- *Professional who knows and understands your child's needs.* This could include your *private* (never someone who works for the school district) occupational or speech therapist, psychologist, or anyone who directly works with your child and understands his needs.

- *Family friend who knows and understands your child's needs.* Always refer to this person as your "advocate." It gives him or her more credibility. This person should have a communication style that complements yours such as being more outgoing if you are shy, or able to step in if you cry. I would discourage the use in this role of another parent whose child receives services within the same district. If there is conflict with staff, they may later experience backlash as a result of advocating for you.

- *Professional with an alphabet of letters behind her name.* Even if this person doesn't know your child well (or at all), but her job is to advocate on behalf of children, this is still an excellent choice. Make sure you're on the same page ahead of time though. You don't want to be blindsided by your own advocate!

It's preferable not to just have ONE advocate. Keep a back-up in mind. I always have more than one in reserve who understands my child's disability. Also, as mentioned, choose someone who complements your communication style. For example, if you are generally an excellent speaker, but not a good detail person, your advocate can help keep you on track and also take notes. If speaking is not your strong point, your advocate can be your mouthpiece, especially if things get rocky and you become upset. The ideal advocate can step in and take over if you are unable to

proceed. If there is no one else available, take someone quiet who is a physical support and who will just take notes.

What Does an Advocate Do?

An advocate understands the needs of your child and can speak on your behalf if necessary. He or she can take notes, ask for questions to be repeated, clarify things, make helpful suggestions and, if you wish, be more assertive than you are. An advocate can also give you feedback after the meeting, which gives you extra insight.

How Do You Prepare with Your Advocate?

Write out your goals. Particularly in the case of autism, many parents want to focus on speech/social skills/life skills goals. List the other things that are important to you, and prioritize them because you aren't going to get everything you want. Then discuss the goals and priorities with your advocate, giving him or her a copy. If you do not have time to get together beforehand, communicate by phone or email.

Have Compassion for Yourself

I used to subscribe to the Brave Little Soldier routine. Chin up, chest out, never let them see your weakness. The chest-out part wasn't so difficult for me, and keeping my emotions all tidy and under wraps was easy too, at first. From the get-go I was the perfect disability mom. I spoke with the appropriate degree of both concern and detachment about my child's needs and I smiled a lot just so people would know it really wasn't all that bad. Really! I'm fine. I've got it perfectly under control.

I heard about other parents breaking down in tears during school meetings and I was shocked. How could they lose it like that? They wouldn't be taken seriously or respected. The staff will smell blood and go after them like sharks, I thought. Well, I was about to face my worst nightmare. I began to fray around the edges near Christmas, a particularly difficult time of year for my kids. Incidents at school led to multiple frustrated phone conversations with the principal, complete with thinly veiled sobbing. It got worse. The same week I had an hour-long appointment crammed in a tiny developmental disability office with all three kids underfoot, desperately trying to keep them from tearing the place apart while the new case worker was learning how to fill out the paperwork to get me some much-needed respite. I must've apologized one too many times because she said, "I know it must be hard to have three children with disabilities." I instantly burst into tears. My *third* child hadn't been diagnosed yet.

The worst was yet to come. Twice in one year I had to leave the IEP meeting because I was crying. I ran to the ladies room, tried to compose myself and returned for another round. But they weren't victim tears; they were passionate tears as I fought on behalf of my children. I finally just gave up and didn't try to hide them even as I felt my face turn hot, my nose running, my voice quavering.

I wouldn't say this is the best technique, and certainly not one I purposely strive for, but it worked miracles. Most people prefer you to put on a happy face, not for your sake, but for theirs. They don't want to feel uncomfortable, to have to consider what life is really like for your family. Showing true emotion reminds them to have compassion. Compassion for the parent, compassion for the child. Yes, there are probably people who will smugly think, "Well, no wonder her kids have problems, just look at her!" But there are also people, like my son's educational assistant, Linda, who said to me after one particularly emotional meeting, "You're my hero."

Fighting with spirit and passion, with deep emotion, doesn't mean your judgment is clouded. It doesn't mean you are less than those professionals who sit there dry-eyed and sure they know what is best for YOUR child. It means that you, more than anyone, feel the depth of your child's needs and are most invested in meeting them. It means that you are plugged in.

Chapter 6

Sanctuary:

Tools for Creating a
Comfortable Home
Environment

Home is a sanctuary from the outside world for most of us, but even more so for kids like ours. It is extremely important that we create a place where they feel accepted, and where their needs will be understood and met.

What does the perfect Asperger Syndrome environment look like? Every home is as unique as the family that lives there, but there are some common tools that can create comfort for all of us. This chapter will take a multi-pronged approach to help you make your home into a sanctuary for all members of your family.

Tools for Transitions

One of the most common problems Asperger Parents experience is the transitions their kids have to make from one activity to another; this includes such things as leaving and arriving home. Our family refers to these bumpy transitions as "re-entry," likening it to the space shuttle having to withstand the treacherous outside forces of re-entering the atmosphere in order to arrive safely home. Lacking the proper equipment, in this case, effective tools, means you might get burned. But once again, with the right tools in hand, on most days you'll sail right through it relatively unscathed.

Picture Schedules

Visual aids are extremely helpful for most children with Asperger Syndrome, and for their parents too! They literally say in black and white what to expect next.

Picture schedules provide a good combination of structure, which helps ease transitions of all types. The more our kids know what is going to happen, the better they are able to master their environment, which eventually fosters independence. It also removes the parent from the equation somewhat; it is the picture schedule telling the child to do the task instead of the parent. This can reduce conflict.

Morning. Start out the day on the right foot by providing a morning schedule for your child. It eliminates the early-morning rush by moving things along in a concise, predictable manner. Both the parent and the child become less frazzled in the last-minute rush.

Good Morning, Morgan!

What Do I Do Next, Mama?

Before we added a picture schedule to our son Tom's morning routine, it was a constant struggle. He was uncooperative and I became impatient. Neither of us was in the best frame of mind to start our day after that! He was 8 years old when we instituted using this tool, but at first I was wondering if it was more trouble than it was worth. This is what it was like.

Tom, "What do I do, Mama?"

Me, "Look at your picture schedule."

Tom, "It says 'Take off pajamas.' He takes off pajamas and stands shivering.

Tom, "What do I do next, Mama?"

Me, "Look at your picture schedule."

Tom reads, "Take off underpants." Takes off underpants, and shivers more.

Me, hurriedly, "Tom, look at your picture schedule."

Tom reads, "Put on underpants." We are both a little relieved.

Tom, "What do I do next, Mama?"

This continued until he was fully dressed, ate breakfast, groomed, had his coat and backpack on and was ready to get on the bus. I would shut the door and groan, thinking, "This is supposed to make LESS work for me?" But there were fewer conflicts, so I stuck it out. Over time he was able to attend to the schedule with only an occasional prompt. Then, he was able to read TWO directions at once, followed by knowing the next step without having to look. Eventually, the schedule gathered dust as he got himself ready for school without any prompting. Once in a while we run into a sluggish period where we dust it off again; it's always there if we need it.

Some people say that picture schedules create dependency, but I would argue that it's quite the opposite. It gives the child a tool that allows him to work independently on his own and feel good about his accomplishments.

Morgan's Afternoon Schedule

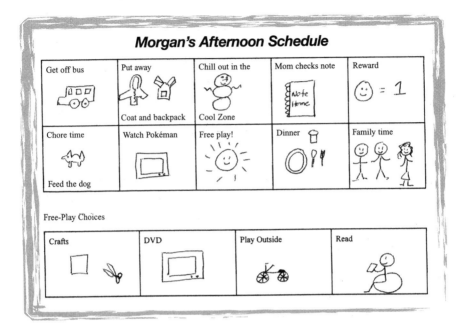

Get off bus	Put away	Chill out in the	Mom checks note	Reward
	Coat and backpack	Cool Zone		☺ = 1
Chore time	Watch Pokémon	Free play!	Dinner	Family time
Feed the dog				

Free-Play Choices

Crafts	DVD	Play Outside	Read

Morgan's Night Schedule

10 MINUTES		
Begin countdown	Take medication	Brush your teeth
Use bathroom	Take off clothes	Put on pajamas
Choose a book	Hop into bed	Storytime!
Hug and kiss good night	Listen to music	Zzzzzz

Afternoon. Many parents have found that keeping a predictable schedule can ease home transitions. Building in a cushion of comfort time the moment the child comes home from school is an important component in reducing stress for all. This can include such things as a home base (explained below), and activities and snacks to which your child responds positively. *Note:* Expectations should be kept low, and any changes should be implemented into the schedule with as much notice as possible.

Night. More about bedtime transitions will be discussed in the sleep section; however, it is important to reinforce the idea of creating a predictable schedule right through bedtime. As in other situations throughout the day, it prepares your child for what is for many AS kids the most difficult transition: sleep.

After-School Reward Time

Many parents set up a predictable reward every day at the same time. If you elect to do so, be sure to include it in the child's schedule. There are a couple of ways to institute such a system.

For school behavior. This is based upon the information received from school-home communication. Every day a certain behavior or task at school reaps the reward when the child comes home.

After a task is performed. In this case it is usually best to give the child time to transition home before requiring him to complete a task. As stated in Chapter 2, rewards are highly motivating. Kids may be willing to do "chores" of your choosing, knowing that there is a predictable reward in their very immediate future. For many families, these "chores" are not what you'd traditionally expect. Instead they want to motivate their child to do things some of us would find enjoyable, but the child does not. This might include playing with a sibling, going for a family walk or reading a book together that the child finds "boring." After he gets over the initial resistance, he may actually enjoy it. Or not! But again, it develops a positive habit.

A Hiding Place

Children naturally seem to gravitate toward little crannies, forts and secret places. It is crucial to provide a specific place within the home for our AS kids where they can withdraw to relax and restore themselves in such times as easing the transition from school, when they are beginning to rumble or any time they feel the need. This is sometimes referred to as a "home base." In Asperger Syndrome and Difficult Moments *(Myles & Southwick, 2005), Amanda Lautenschlager and her son, Ethan, are credited with the term "cool zone."*

It's important to note that it is not "time-out." Going to the cool zone or home base is not a punishment. It is a place for your child to feel safe, comfortable, and pull himself together. Don't force a child to go to his home base; however, you may encourage, or even reward him for doing so if he appears to need it.

From time to time, ask if you can "come in" and join him. If he says yes, then count yourself lucky. He might be more willing to talk with you in his own space.

Suggested hiding places include:

- *Behind a piece of furniture, such as the sofa pulled out from the wall, or alongside the bed.*

- *A big cardboard box that he can decorate. Markers can be provided for drawing on the "walls" while he is relaxing.*

- *A closet, open or closed. Never put a child in a dark or enclosed space, but if he wants to go there, allow him to do so.*

- *Blanket-over-a-table fort. How often does your family actually eat in the dining room these days? Put that fancy table to good use; make a blanket fort.*

Organizational Tools

It is said that kids with AS have either the messiest or the cleanest desks at school. The same goes for their rooms at home. They either have everything perfectly organized, or they have seemingly no ability to remember where an object is the second it leaves their hand. The latter kind of child not only has no idea where his coat and backpack are, worse yet, he loses even the important things in his life – his favorite toy and his very important cards. Failure to find these things can cause hysteria, even in parents! We know what can happen, so even if we look calm, we have one predominant thought, "OH NO!" Once our kids start that rage cycle, it can ruin their (and your) entire evening.

For kids like this we have to keep on top of things. If you're not an organized person (I speak for myself here!), learning basic organizational skills will ultimately make your life a lot easier. Here are some suggestions that have helped in our house.

Reduce Visual Clutter

The more stuff they have to visually attend to, the harder it is for kids with AS to see what they are looking for.

Organize toys in lidded bins. I recommend you keep the bins in a central location where you are more likely to keep control over them. If they are in the child's room out of your sight, you're more likely to be stepping on Legos when you wake the kid up in the morning. (Legos seem to be particularly popular among our kids, so we'll use that as an example.)

Use one at a time. If you have more than one kind of building set, you'll have a big mess on your hands if you let them have them all out at once (written by someone who has spent a major part of her life sorting Legos and K'nex). Set up a system where the children are only allowed to have one kind out at a time and only in a specified location. (Unless all the other toys are put away, it's not always a good idea to let them do this in their room where there is greater chance of pieces getting lost.)

Pour toys onto a blanket. In our home we pour our very large collection of Legos onto a thin blanket, so when it is time to put them away, an adult can help the child pick up the blanket and pour them back into the bin. We call this "Making a burrito." Although pieces will inevitably spread out, it still makes cleaning up less overwhelming for everyone.

Eliminate knick-knacks. Like delicate and fragile things? Then I suggest you go back in time and not have children! Not only do these things add to the already chaotic nature of the environment your child attends to, they are prime targets during meltdowns. Put Great Grandma's china some place out of sight until the kid grows up and moves out.

Keep the mess contained. If you have a family room, then make that toy or craft central. We have a craft table that at any one time is covered with playdough, cardboard contraptions, piles of papers, and the like. We keep our kids well stocked with glue, tape and string. Is it messy? You bet! Are my kids creative and generally happy? Yes! A little tip: Keep a box to toss these various creations in, and from time to time, under cover of dark, slip the older ones out of the house on trash day. Shhh, don't tell!

House vs. Home

Guess what? You've got a kid! Therefore, you've got clutter. It sounds like a contradiction of the above section to say that you have to accept a certain amount of mess in the house along with the existence of the creature known as "the child," but life is a constant contradiction, is it not? Reality is, kids are messy, loud and generally not that interested in how lovely your house appears for guests – or even that less mess helps you maintain your sanity.

If you're running all over hollering at them over being (normal) messy kids all the time, it's not a peaceful home for either of you. I used to have a kitchen floor you literally could have eaten off of. I got over it! My motto now is, "My house is clean enough to be healthy and dirty enough to be happy." Do you want a house, or do you want a home? My guess is the latter. Organization helps you keep things under reasonable control, but it doesn't eliminate the fact that you have a kid. So stop stressing.

Using Visuals to Our Advantage

Our kids respond to visual supports and, as previously mentioned, so do most dads! Once you've taken the time to set things up, it almost eliminates the requirement of having to use actual brain cells. Plus it leads to kids becoming more independent because they can manage more things on their own. It builds habits, which, as we know, create new brain pathways. It's also yet another example of short-term effort for long-term gain. Here are a few examples.

Pictures. Backpacks, coats and shoes strung all over? Put up a picture of these items where they should go, and kids will learn to match the item to the location. A habit is born.

Labels. Clearly label drawers by each item of clothing to go there. For example, top drawer: pajamas, underwear, socks. This makes it easier for your child to get dressed independently without you having to pick out his clothes. If he doesn't read, use pictures. Tape them on with heavy clear packing tape. Will this new-found independence sometimes lead to interesting fashion combinations? Absolutely. But have you seen how other kids dress these days? They've got nothing on our kids! My other favorite benefit to labels is that my husband can now remember where to put things without prompting.

Sensory Pleasures

Our kids have intense sensory needs. Suggestions for creative ways to address this are discussed later in *Family Sensory Activities*, but it also rates a strong mention when discussing the home in general. Notice how it seems that everything our AS child needs is expensive, such as vitamins and alternative treatments? And then there are his sensory needs. You could build your own occupational therapy center right in your home and equip it with a squeeze machine and sky gym. Certainly, the therapy center where our kids receive occupational therapy has a multitude of important tools, including such things. In reality, that's generally out of the scope of what parents can provide at home. However, there *are* many inexpensive ways to help your child meet his sensory needs. Here are a few examples.

Fidgets

These are small, usually pretty, disposable gadgets for kids to fiddle with. As annoying as I personally find it, my kids pay a whole lot *more* attention to me when they look like they aren't because they have something to move from hand to hand. A couple of favorites at our house are sticky hands, prickly or squishy balls. The most nerve-wracking for me, but one of the most helpful, include whistles and toys that require blowing. A little noisy, yes. Relaxing for our kids and therefore worth it? Also yes. Although you can purchase these items at the local store, the Oriental Trading Company (www.orientaltrading.com) is a whole lot cheaper, literally by the dozen. And you'll need 'em. They ARE breakable. Oh, and a little bonus, they make great rewards.

Playdough, Clay and Putty

The pushing, tugging, and squishing of these things is incredibly relaxing for our kids. And frankly, have you tried it? It feels gooooood.

Rice Sock

This is my favorite, and that's why I steal it often. This is so simple that it's got what I call the "duh" factor to it. Get your kids to help you make it. Here's what you do: Fill a tube sock with approximately three cups of rice, tie a TIGHT knot in the end – and ta-da!

Now what on earth do you do with it? It can be a weight to use on your child's shoulders to help him relax during a transition, such as upon arriving home after school. It also has the cool component, an hour in the freezer and ahhhh. And even more impressive, three minutes in the microwave and you've got a flexible and portable heating pad.

Beanbag Chair

You have to purchase this, but it has long-lasting value. The down-side to this wonderful "tool" is that it requires filling with styrofoam beads. If you haven't done this, you may be wondering what the big deal is. If you attempt to dump the beads directly from the clear plastic bag into the zippered beanbag shell, you will instantly have a lesson in the marvels of static cling. As delightful as this is for your children, trust me, you won't find it nearly as amusing when it insistently continues to cling to *you* … a week later. Here's a little tip: Stuff the entire plastic bag into the beanbag shell, rip a hole in the plastic, zip the beanbag shut and squish it around. It'll work itself out eventually. A second suggestion is to spray the pellets with static cling spray.

What's so great about a beanbag chair? Who knows? Maybe it's the satisfying sound it makes, the way you can sort of settle down into it. But I can't tell you how many times I've found my children UNDER it, especially when they are rumbling or recovering.

Sensory Snacks

Although many of our kids are limited in their diets, they often seem to have their mouths on everything else! Providing snacks from their "sensory diet" is not only comforting, it helps them orient to doing other tasks. Chewy snacks such as red ropes or jerky are helpful for focusing, so they're a good snack when you want attentiveness. Crunchy snacks such as popcorn or chips, or in a perfect world – carrot sticks (if your kid will eat them, mine won't!) – are alerting. The same goes for sour candies, such as Lemonheads. So when our kids are dragging a little, this might be the perfect pick-me-up. They even work on parents!

These are just a few examples. Your child's occupational therapist can provide specific suggestions for various activities and times of the day. Many kids have these items with them and learn how to use them to self-regulate.

A Word About Electronics

Many Asperger kids are completely taken with videogames and computers. Parents report one of their biggest struggles is getting their child "off" these things and transitioning to another activity. Here are a few suggestions.

- *Don't have them. Many parents do not to allow their children to have electronic games at all.*

- *Limit access. You may choose to only allow your child play a game in the car, for example.*

- *Schedule use. Provide a set time once a day with a time limit. This can also be used as a reward, such as 30 minutes of videogames or computer in exchange for completing homework or chores, or simply as a matter of course set in stone on the daily schedule.*

The key in managing our kids and electronics is to have clear guidelines. Whether it is a "rule" or it is put into the schedule, do it consistently. Make it clear ahead of time that they will lose this privilege if they do not cooperate and quit in a timely manner. Remember, none of these things works if we use the electronics as a babysitter. The longer our kids are on it, the more difficult it is for them to transition off.

Food Wars

Parents are often told that if they don't make their kids eat green beans and broccoli, they are bad parents. Who says so? Even a former president of the United States owned up to hating broccoli. I agree, it would be great if our kids just loved to eat green veggies and if we all ate a perfectly rounded diet. But let's face reality. Even many typically developing children are picky, preferring fast food to a homemade casserole. Many a parent has put his foot down and said, "You are not leaving this table until you clean your plate!" But at what cost?

The national Center on Addiction and Substance Abuse (CASA) at

Columbia University released survey results that highlight the importance of the family dinner. Accordingly to chairman and president Joseph F. Califano Jr., "The survey finds that the more often children have dinner with their parents, the less likely they are to smoke, drink or use illegal drugs." Statistically, teenagers who ate dinner with their families were 31% less likely to engage in these behaviors. Furthermore, the study reports that children who ate dinner with their families four or more times per week were less likely to be bored, did well in school and handled stress better than their peers.

These findings are powerful motivation for families to break bread together in an atmosphere of warmth and acceptance. If you are battling over food and an aura of stress hangs over the dinner table, it defeats the purpose. Set aside traditional presumptions about what dinner should look like and instead think of what purpose you would like the family time together to serve. Then consider why we feel so strongly about what our children eat in the first place.

What's It REALLY About?

It's important to think about why we want our kids to eat things that are extremely unpleasant to them. Is it solely because we're worried about nutrition? Is it that we enjoy something and we are afraid our child will miss out on the same enjoyment? Or is it because it is part of our culture and their rejection makes us fear they will reject all of who we are? How do we feel when we make Great Grandma's special stew and our child vomits it up after one bite or plain refuses to eat it at all?

Most food wars are not about food at all, but the associations food holds for us. Food is at the heart of who we are; it is a reflection of our culture. Think about the foods you love most and why. Is it apple pie? If yes, perhaps it's because it reminds you of happy holidays with your grandparents. Pancakes? Leisurely Sunday mornings when you were a child. Even if it's McDonald's french fries, there's probably a memory associated that makes them especially tasty. So when a child sits down at the family dinner table and rejects the food that is familiar to us and, worse yet, if we have made it with our own loving hands in our sincerest desire to care for our family, it can feel as if the child is rejecting us, our tradition, even our values.

Before you consider yourself mortally hurt and wounded, remember it is just food. Our children are not making a conscious choice to reject it, or us. They are just having a physiological reaction to the sight and the smell of the food. It's not personal.

Are we insisting our children eat foods they find distasteful because we are worried about how others will react? People will have opinions and make comments, but if someone is grumbling about your child's food intake, that's the least of your worries. Above all, it is your responsibility to make decisions that are in his best interest, including this one. For the most part, if you seem ambivalent, that's when people call you into question. If you are firm in your parenting beliefs, not only will you likely be criticized less often, you'll feel less concerned when you are.

Calling a Truce: Tools for Having an Enjoyable Family Dinner

I'm not suggesting that you let your kids eat whatever they want. If it was completely up to my children, they would eat candy for breakfast, lunch and dinner, with an ice cream chaser! Instead, try some of these suggestions.

Cover the bases. Try to find at least one item in all four food groups that your child will eat, and let him eat it. If you're worried he's missing something nutritionally, give him a multivitamin to be sure he's covered.

Work on one goal at a time. As in many other cases in our family, we've found that it is better to focus on one issue at a time. If you are very concerned about your child's diet, then make that the current priority, but let off the pressure in another area of the child's life to reduce the amount of stress your child is experiencing.

Offer rewards. Allow the child to make the choice to eat something new and receive some compensation for it. A reward can be anything from getting a token, dessert, special treat, or watching a cartoon on a school night.

Keep it to yourself and see what happens. Other families choose not to pressure children about eating certain foods, but continue to have them present at the dinner table. If you are eating something that is on your child's banned list, just by seeing it up close, eventually he may become desensitized to the sight and smell. However, if it is truly distressing to your child, don't put the broccoli right next to HIS plate.

Let it solve itself. As they mature, even our kids can become more flexible. If your child is only eating oatmeal at age four, it doesn't mean he'll only eat oatmeal for the rest of his life.

Do a little detective work. Discuss with your child what makes some foods intolerable for him. He may not be able to express specifically what he doesn't like about it, but it's worth a try. It may be the taste, the texture, seasoning or visual appeal.

Taking a Closer Look

Taste. *Vegetables may taste bitter to our kids with highly attuned taste buds. Try offering the sweeter vegetables such as carrots, corn, peas.*

Texture. *Your child may refuse mashed potatoes because you've used the hand masher and there are too many lumps. You may both discover that he is willing to eat and even enjoy mashed potatoes that are carefully whipped with a hand mixer.*

Seasoning. *It may be that something is too salty/spicy or too bland. A recent KFC commercial said, "You can't have too much flavor!" To which our son Kito replied, "Yes, you can!!"*

Visual. *He might refuse something with mixed ingredients, such as a casserole, but eat exactly the same items if served separately. There may be a couple of reasons for this. One is he can't "trust" what is in the dish because he can't clearly see all the ingredients. Another reason may be related to having more than one taste or texture in the mouth at the same time. Some parents have found that the best way to get their child to eat a whole plateful of food is to serve it up on a plate with dividers so the foods don't "touch" each other. This allows the child to clearly see what is in his dinner, and there's no chance of "cross-contamination" of one food with another!*

The more you ease up on your food expectations, the more flexible your child often becomes. He will build a greater sense of trust in you because he isn't expecting to be forced to eat something that is disagreeable to him. The decreased anxiety alone will make dinnertime more enjoyable.

Note: Some parents find that a gluten-free casein-free (GFCF) diet makes an enormous difference in their children's lives. For others, it doesn't seem to make any difference. This is something that can only be determined by examining the information published, such as at www.gfcfdiet.com, about this subject and then deciding whether or not you want to make the effort. It is a big decision, but if it works, it may well be worth the trouble.

Gravy Purgatory

I'm a fabulous cook, just ask anyone … except my children. But there is one thing I can make that soothes my children's picky appetites and every other discriminating dinner guest alike: I am famous for my mashed potatoes and gravy. I won't let you in on all of my secrets, but I'll reveal this much: There is butter and cream cheese involved. However, I suspect that there will be a penalty to pay for my overenthusiastic mashed potato and gravy pushing – I'll probably end up in Gravy Purgatory.

I'll be standing in line on my way into heaven and St. Peter will pull me and a bunch of grey-haired ladies aside and say, "Come with me, please." We'll receive an accounting of all the people we sent to pre-mature deaths from artery-clogging cholesterol from our gravy and fixings, followed by spending an eternity swapping recipes. Maybe I'll finally learn to knit! Instead of the people I left behind praying to get me out, they'll be sitting around at Thanksgiving dinner saying, "Damn! I miss Mama's gravy!" Not a bad way to be remembered.

Is Your Family Getting Enough Sleep?

Sleep is a major issue to parents of children with AS – who is getting it, who is not, and what they are doing about it. Many kids with AS experience sleep problems starting from an early age and, consequently, so do their parents! Lack of sleep affects everyone, including parents, who may not be as patient with their children as they would like to be.

Why Do AS Kids Have Sleep Issues?

When you consider the major characteristics of ASD, it should come as no major surprise that many children with AS have sleep problems.

Difficulty with transitions. As we know, AS children often have difficulty transitioning from one activity to another. Sleep is no different. Awake-to-asleep and sleep-to-awake cycles are hard to manage. Our kids like to stay where they are when they are comfortable; they don't see any reason why they should move on to something they might not enjoy quite as much!

Overstimulation. While the demands of school are exhausting, they can also be overstimulating. We've all experienced days when we've had so much going on that instead of sleeping we toss and turn all night. This is a regular way of life for many AS children.

Anxiety. Many children and adults with AS suffer from anxiety, often due to the stress they experience throughout their day created by the high expectations and demands of the outside world. For example, they may be aware of their social problems, or worried about not doing well in school, and when they are lying in bed worried and anxious, that is not conducive to sleep.

Underlying related neurological issues. They often say in medicine, "If you hear hoofbeats in the night, look for horses not zebras." In other words, look for the obvious causes first. However, if all lesser interventions have failed to help your child sleep, he may need to be evaluated for other neurological issues, including having an EEG to check for seizure disorders.

Grateful, But Not Volunteering for More

The other night during bedtime prayers my son Tom said, "Thank you for giving me Aspergers." Afterward when I asked him about it, he said matter-of-factly, "It's a gift really." "Why?" "Because it allows me to complete challenges that other people would find too diffi-

cult." I asked for specifics, but all he could say was, "I cannot think of an example right now. I just know it to be true in my heart."

*I could not make this stuff up! Maybe I should be saying a few more thanks. Thanks for giving all three of my kids Asperger Syndrome? Hmmm, maybe not! God might then decide to send me a fourth, and I think that should be shared with some **other** well-deserving family. Only three per customer!*

Tools for Tucking Them in for the Night

Several simple tools may help overcome your child's sleeping problem, or at least ease the transition and create an atmosphere of comfort and security. Below are a few suggestions that have helped many families, including ours.

Keep a routine and use a picture schedule. As mentioned repeatedly, AS kids generally adjust more easily if they know what to expect. It gives them a feeling of control, even if it is something they do not want to do. It cuts down on bedtime conflicts.

Keep stimulating activities to a minimum and wind down the day toward bedtime. For most kids, this includes limiting television and videogames. A child may look calm while watching TV, but the activities he experiences remain inside his brain for a while, and he may have trouble discharging them before sleep.

Take a look at what your child is wearing. One child may want to wear a lot of clothes to bed, another may want to sleep in his underwear despite chilly temperatures. We don't share the same skins as these kids, and they feel things differently than we do. Some kids need heavy clothes because they don't want any blankets touching them. Others wear almost nothing because the heavy weighted blanket they prefer is too hot, or maybe they want to feel its texture against their skin. It is rarely a battle important enough to wage unless you live at the North Pole and your child is in actual danger of becoming a popsicle. In the case of children who cannot communicate their needs, use your powers of observation, trial and error.

The following might sound like a day spa YOU would like to visit! Implement soothing activities into the bedtime routine, such as:

- *Calming music.* Some parents opt for classical music, but that's not the only choice. Many families play soft rock or country music – parents may enjoy this, too! The key is that the music is calm and not upbeat close to bedtime.

- *Water.* For some children water is soothing, and an aromatherapy bath might help. (Obviously, if your child hates the feeling of water and freaks out at bath time, this would not a good choice!)

- *Back rub.* Many a child has fallen to sleep while his back was being rubbed. Experiment with different kinds of pressure. Many kids with AS like the heavier pressure because it's not so tickle-y.

- *Warm drinks such as chamomile tea.* If the child refuses to drink it due to taste, try sweetening it with a spoonful of honey. Have him sip it as he winds down the evening so it has taken effect by bedtime.

- *Weighted blanket.* Many children enjoy the deep-pressure feeling of a heavy blanket to relieve stress. You can purchase weighted blankets, but most parents create their own by making a heavy cover for an existing comforter. Don't sew? Try merely stuffing a duvet with TWO comforters.

- *Talking over the day to discharge worries and reassure the child.* This is not the time to lecture; it is time to listen. If your child has difficulty telling you what is bothering him, talk about the things that you love about him, praise him for small successes he had that day.

Something VERY Important

The other night I was firmly insisting that little bodies settle down, be quiet and go to sleep. Tom burst out, "But Mama! I have to tell Kito something VERY important!" I sighed and said, "Okay, just one more thing." He sat up and said cheerfully, "Hey, Kito! Kito! Kito! You know what? You know what? You know what? The Egyptians removed the brains of the deceased before placing them in the tomb. Through their noses! PIECE BY PIECE." To which Kito reacted, not with horror, but with absolute glee. Not your usual bedtime story, is it? But viva la Special Interest! I turned off the light and pretended not to hear the LOUD whispering that went on for quite a while after that, and smiled contentedly to myself.

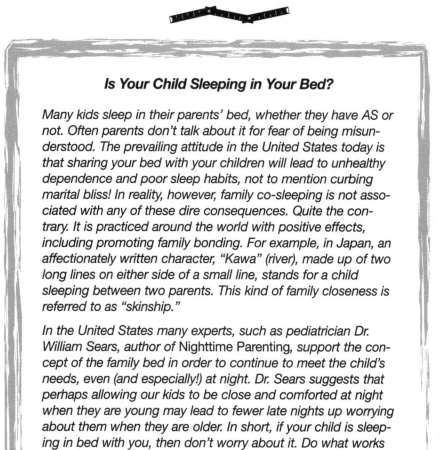

Is Your Child Sleeping in Your Bed?

Many kids sleep in their parents' bed, whether they have AS or not. Often parents don't talk about it for fear of being misunderstood. The prevailing attitude in the United States today is that sharing your bed with your children will lead to unhealthy dependence and poor sleep habits, not to mention curbing marital bliss! In reality, however, family co-sleeping is not associated with any of these dire consequences. Quite the contrary. It is practiced around the world with positive effects, including promoting family bonding. For example, in Japan, an affectionately written character, "Kawa" (river), made up of two long lines on either side of a small line, stands for a child sleeping between two parents. This kind of family closeness is referred to as "skinship."

In the United States many experts, such as pediatrician Dr. William Sears, author of Nighttime Parenting, support the concept of the family bed in order to continue to meet the child's needs, even (and especially!) at night. Dr. Sears suggests that perhaps allowing our kids to be close and comforted at night when they are young may lead to fewer late nights up worrying about them when they are older. In short, if your child is sleeping in bed with you, then don't worry about it. Do what works for your family.

A discussion of sleep would not be complete without mentioning medication. Administering medication to help your child sleep is an extremely personal issue, and you should discuss it with your child's doctor. In general, the best choice is to start out with the least intervention such as the tools suggested earlier, and if things do not resolve themselves, perhaps consider the next step of discussing it with your doctor. Many parents hesitate to put their children on medication, but many discover after they have made a well-thought-out decision to do so that their children sleep better and, consequently, behavior and performance in school often improve. Also, parents who get more sleep are able to be more patient with their children.

Medication

You've developed parenting tools, created a supportive environment for your AS child and tapped all of your resources, but your child continues to have behavior issues. Perhaps there is another component that needs to be treated medically. For example, many children, adolescents and adults with Asperger Syndrome suffer from anxiety and depression. It's also not uncommon for children who have AS to carry a secondary diagnosis, such as attention deficit hyperactive disorder or bipolar disorder, that behavior supports alone cannot solve.

This is when parents turn to their medical providers for additional answers. There are ever-increasingly effective medications for treating the symptoms associated with Asperger Syndrome and other neurological disorders. Giving medication to children is a decision that must be weighed carefully with your medical care provider, preferably a pediatric psychiatrist. If this is the option you choose, here are a few tips that can make it easier.

Managing Medication

Parents struggle over the decision to give their children medication, and then it turns out that it opens up a whole other can of worms. It's one more thing they have to manage. But as in many other things, a well-established routine, for you this time, pays off over the long run.

Educate yourself about the side effects of the medications your child is taking. Psychiatrists, in particular, are excellent at explaining what to watch for. Medication inserts can also be helpful, but they are often hard to understand. If you have questions, never hesitate to call your doctor or ask your pharmacist. Do not feel foolish about asking questions; it's the smart parents who ask questions!

Educate your child about his medications – what they look like and their dosages. It is empowering for children to know what the specific medications are for. They may be less resistant to taking something if they understand why. Also, although it should not be their responsibility, many children have caught mistakes before the wrong medication was administered to them. Of course, never assume your child will be able to do this. Medications are ALWAYS the adults' responsibility.

Give medication at a consistent time. This is very important. Therefore, make sure you always have at least one dose of the child's medication with you. Many families find themselves delayed by circumstances beyond their control, and when they get home it is well past the time when their child was supposed to receive his meds, and as a result there may be behavior issues.

If your child must take medication at school, send the correct amount for one week plus one extra day. This overlap allows you a cushion in case you forget to send it.

Develop a check-off or other system to prevent double dosing or missing medication. This prevents guesswork if you don't know if the other parent or caregiver has given it, or frankly, if you just forget. One method is to have a weekly pill case in which you put all the daily medications for the week. Another option is to have a medication checklist, simply a chart with boxes to check by the name of each medication and time it is given. Both parents can easily see if the box is checked and know the child has already been medicated.

Post a list of medications, dosage and times to administer them on the refrigerator. This way all adults in the home have access to the information and there is less chance of making a mistake. This is also important if your child has an outside adult take care of him.

Choose one specific day of the week to check if you are running low on medication. This is especially important if you are dealing with more than one prescription. Mondays are a good day because it's easy to remember and if you are out of refills, it gives your pharmacy plenty of time to contact your doctor's office. No one wants to be caught out of medication on a weekend!

Ask the doctor's office to call in medications to the pharmacy ahead of time. That way they will be waiting for you when you go to pick them up. This saves you the stress of waiting for them with your child.

Order refills by phone, if convenient. If you are out of refills, most computerized systems have an option that allows you to request they contact your doctor for a new RX. This speeds up the process.

If Your Child Refuses to Take His Medication

It is not a surprise that many kids with AS are reluctant to swallow pills; after all, they are often picky eaters and don't like to swallow many foods! This can be frustrating, and even dangerous. Most drugs must be taken consistently to have the intended effect, and many cannot be stopped suddenly because of the risk of a rebound reaction, especially most antidepressants and mood stabilizers.

Many families, including my own, have faced this situation, here are a few suggestions to help you.

Tell your doctor your child has difficulty swallowing pills. He or she may be able to substitute a sprinkle that can be mixed in food or a liquid that is easier to take; some medications even come as dissolving tablets.

Find out if pills can be split or ground to make them easier to get down. Check with your doctor or pharmacist because some medications, such as time-release pills, can become dangerous if broken before they are swallowed.

Talk to your pharmacist about alternatives. "Compound pharmacies" can take almost any medication and create a liquid form of it. In some cases they can also add in flavors to make it more palatable. Check your *Yellow Pages*.

Offer rewards. When all else fails, you know what they say, "A spoonful of sugar makes the medicine go down!" A little treat, like a Hershey's kiss, might be just the thing to encourage the reluctant child to swallow something "yucky."

Change your approach. Think about how you are talking to your child when you are giving him his medication. Don't make it a question, because then he is likely to say, "No!" And don't make it a demand either, because it will likely have the same result. Try stating it plainly as a fact, "Take your medication and THEN we are going to have a snack." Or, "First you take your medication and THEN you can watch TV." If it is a natural sequence of events and not a challenge, your child might be more cooperative.

Think about where and when you administer meds. If you call your child into the kitchen to take his meds in the middle of his TV show, he obviously won't be happy about it. Timing can be everything. For some kids bringing the medication to them meets with better results because it requires less effort on their part. Stay there and make sure they swallow though!

Put it on the picture schedule. This is perhaps the least confrontational way to administer medication because it is the picture schedule telling the child it's time for his pill, not you. Fewer verbal instructions with more visual reinforcements often work wonders at preventing resistance.

Many medications have side effects and, again, are best prescribed by pediatric psychiatrists because they are most informed about the benefits and risks. Every child reacts differently, so there is no way to know exactly how your child will respond. Also, often there is an adjustment period to find the right medication, or combination of medications. This is why it is important to have a good working relationship with your child's doctor, so if things go awry, you can trust her to quickly resolve it.

By the sound of things, medications may not seem worth the trouble! While it's true that it is an added responsibility for you to take care of and worry about, for many children medication can literally make the difference between being functional or not. However, remember, there is no magic pill; medication is only one tool in your arsenal of options.

Matters of Hygiene, Because Hygiene Matters

Hygiene is a major social issue. Things are supposed to smell nice and have a neat appearance, especially our bodies. People with autism spectrum disorders are already at a disadvantage socially; if we want our children to fit in and be accepted by others, we must teach them to maintain at least minimal standards of cleanliness. Yet, many parents struggle with their AS kids when it comes to matters of hygiene. Here's an example many Asperger Parents will recognize.

Bath Time Blues

"Drew!" his mom calls, "bath time!" Drew doesn't answer. "Drew!" His mother calls again. Silence. Mom starts to get annoyed. Why doesn't that boy answer? It's getting late; they are expected to go out to dinner with friends, and Drew is dawdling AGAIN. She does a search through every room in the house while calling his name, finally checking under his bed. Yep, there he is. "Drew!" Her voice is firm, "It's BATH TIME, didn't you hear me calling?"

Drew doesn't answer; he is drawing a picture. "Drew!" his mother raises her voice. "Bath time NOW." He starts to whine. "I'm drawing a picture!" His mother sighs, "You can draw the picture later; come right now." He ignores her. Now Drew's mother is getting a little more upset. Her son keeps drawing. "Drew, let's go." As she reach-

es under the bed and pulls him out, he fights her a little, but finally goes reluctantly, looking sullen.

Both of them enter the bathroom already keyed up by the exchange. Drew struggles pulling off his clothes; he can't get his shirt over his head. His mother doesn't say anything, but is impatient. They were already running behind schedule; they don't have much time to get ready. And she wouldn't even have to give him a bath right now, if he didn't have markers all over him. Why isn't that boy more careful? These are her thoughts as she tugs his shirt over his head. Why can't he do these things himself? He's a big boy!

Drew puts one foot in the tub and screams, "It's hot! It's hot! It's hot!" His mom sighs and puts her hand in the water to check, "No it's not, it's just right; get in." He says, "uh uh." Feeling her irritation rising, she adds some cooler water and glances at her watch. In the meantime Drew stands there shivering, "Get in, it's fine." He pauses, "Are you going to wash my hair?" No! Just get in!" Finally, very reluctantly, he gets into the tub, making a face like he's hurt.

This is followed by much splashing about as Drew starts playing in the water as his mother tries to hurry him along. She examines his head more closely and decides that, indeed, she MUST wash his hair. It looks awful! Knowing she's about to face a battle, she reaches for the shampoo. Drew sees her, "NO! You said you weren't going to wash my hair! No! No! No!" Taking deep breaths and trying not to totally lose patience, his mom says as evenly as she can manage, "Drew, we HAVE to wash your hair." "No, I don't want to!" He starts splashing even more frantically in the water. She quickly grabs the shampoo, spilling a bunch as she pours it into her hand, and rubs it on his head as he continues to try to get away from her. "Drew!" she says firmly, "sit still! You're almost fin- ished!" But Drew isn't listening, he's continues, "No! No! No! I don't want to!"

Drew's mom feels terrible about the whole situation, but now she doesn't know what else to do but push through to the end. She tries to get him to lean back so she can rinse his hair, but he won't cooperate. Finally she scoops some water into a cup and pours it over his head, quickly trying to wipe his face with a towel. By now Drew is sobbing, he looks at her like she's drowning him. Drew's mom feels like sobbing too; she's almost as wet as he is as she gets him out of the tub and wraps him up in a towel. Feeling guilty for being so insistent, she thinks, "What else am I supposed to do? He has to have a bath!" Drew is inconsolable although his mom tries to comfort him. He says, "You're a meanie! You lied! You said you weren't going to wash my hair!" His mom cringes. Why does every-thing have to be so hard?

Interpreting Through Eyes of Understanding

Is Drew a bad boy? Is his mom mean? Or are they both just caught in a power struggle complicated by factors beyond their control? Drew's sensory issues are a major factor in how this bath scene unfolds. His mom doesn't understand why her son gets upset, only that he does. And even if she realizes he has sensory issues, it doesn't help her understand what to do about it. She doesn't have the proper tools.

Let's look at the sensory issues involved here.

- Drew may not have heard his mother calling the first several times; he was completely focused on his drawing. He was visu-ally attentive, but not processing auditory stimuli (literally couldn't hear).

- Drew's mom pulled him out from under the bed, causing his senses to go on high alert and click into a fight-or-flight response, with adrenaline already running high.

- Drew had trouble undressing himself, especially because he was being hurried. Pulling his shirt over his head affected his sense of balance, further heightening his sense of uneasiness.

- Although the bath temperature might have been okay for his mother, it was too hot for Drew.

- The shampoo probably felt cold and gooey, which is something that bothers many AS kids.

- Drew was reluctant to lean back to wash his hair because of his poor balance.

- The water being poured over his head literally flooded his senses; he lost his sense of spatial awareness; he was disoriented and afraid.

- Unknown: There might have been other sensory issues in this kind of situation, even though Drew didn't tell his mom. For example, the shampoo scent might be too strong and irritate him – so maybe they need to switch to unscented. Or the light is too bright – they need to change the wattage, or type of bulb used. These are things that can only be discovered by understanding the basic sensory issues that AS children have, plus observation and trial and error with each individual child.

All of these issues – along with the sense of being rushed, Drew's mom getting impatient, their emotions running high – caused this bath time disaster. But what else could Drew's mom do? Is it her fault that her son has these issues? And he *has* to take a bath, right? Of course, Drew's mom has to help her son learn to be clean! She would not be a responsible parent if she didn't, but with proper tools the entire situation could have gone a lot better.

Drew's mom felt frustrated for many reasons. One of them was the rush, but she also had residual feelings from previous events. She went into the situation knowing it would be a battle, feeling conflicted. Her own emotions were running high before bath time even began. It is important for us as parents to change our inner dialogue when faced with potentially difficult situations with our kids.

We need to keep reinforcing what the "right" thing to do is, such as keeping the child's sensory needs in mind, instead of focusing on past events or dire predictions. It's a difficult line sometimes between "thinking ahead" and "predicting failure," but with self-awareness we'll get better at it.

Revisiting Bath Time Using Tools

What are the tools Drew's mom could incorporate into bath time in order to have a more successful outcome next time? You guessed it – priming, predicting, countdown, visual supports, reward, wrap-up. Along with an eye for the sensory issues, these things could have completely changed the experience for both of them.

Priming. Drew's mom regularly reinforces that "Saturday is bath day." She points it out to him on the calendar regularly. It becomes matter of fact; he knows when it will occur.

Predicting. Drew's mom thinks about all the variables regarding bathing. She assembles all the things she will need ahead of time within reach, so she doesn't have to struggle in the moment of the "event."

Countdown. When the time to bathe approaches, Mom reminds Drew of the schedule. She then begins the countdown to when he will go to his bath. She also is mindful of the time he is in the bath, and gives him clear parameters about how long he must endure each stage. For example, she can count down how many rinses it will take for his hair. This gives him a sense of when it will end.

Visual supports. Drew's mom draws a picture of the bathtub on every Saturday of the month on the calendar. She also creates a picture schedule; that is, a list of the things that occur at bath time. Perhaps she even has him help her with it (most kids draw better than we do anyway!). It might say something like: "Take off clothes. Check temperature of water. Get in tub. Play for 10 minutes. Shampoo hair, rinse, get out of tub."

Reward! We cannot forget the most important factor as far as the AS child is concerned! Drew will respond better with a consistent, expected reward. In this case, Drew loves to eat popcorn and watch a movie with his mom after bath time. It is their weekly ritual.

Wrap-up. Drew's mom takes a few minutes to consider what went well this time around and what didn't work, so next time she can make adjustments. She and Drew can also have a brief exchange about it if he's up for it. If not, perhaps they can discuss it at another time; he might be able to give her some feedback about what is hard for him, and what helps.

In addition to the tools, there are a couple of other things to consider in any potentially difficult situation with your AS child, as outlined below.

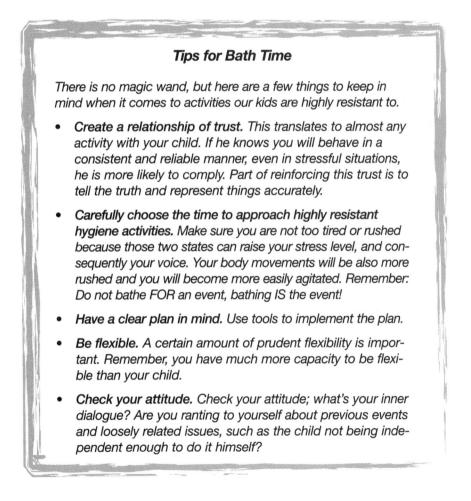

Tips for Bath Time

There is no magic wand, but here are a few things to keep in mind when it comes to activities our kids are highly resistant to.

- **Create a relationship of trust.** *This translates to almost any activity with your child. If he knows you will behave in a consistent and reliable manner, even in stressful situations, he is more likely to comply. Part of reinforcing this trust is to tell the truth and represent things accurately.*

- **Carefully choose the time to approach highly resistant hygiene activities.** *Make sure you are not too tired or rushed because those two states can raise your stress level, and consequently your voice. Your body movements will be also more rushed and you will become more easily agitated. Remember: Do not bathe FOR an event, bathing IS the event!*

- **Have a clear plan in mind.** *Use tools to implement the plan.*

- **Be flexible.** *A certain amount of prudent flexibility is important. Remember, you have much more capacity to be flexible than your child.*

- **Check your attitude.** *Check your attitude; what's your inner dialogue? Are you ranting to yourself about previous events and loosely related issues, such as the child not being independent enough to do it himself?*

Bath Time Revisited

Let's take a look at how things could have unfolded differently using the tools.

Drew's mom checks in on her son, who is playing in his room. "Drew! Remember, it's Saturday, it's bath time at 2:00." Drew says, "Awww! I hate taking a bath!" His mom smiles knowingly, "I know, sorry about that. But we'll make it quick and you can get your reward." Drew goes back to playing.

Half an hour before bath time mom swings by his room, "It's bath time in 30 minutes, Drew." She makes sure he has heard her by leaning down to him face-to-face. "Did you hear me?" He nods and keeps playing. This repeats in perhaps another 15 minutes. Then at 5 minutes, she says, "Drew, it's almost bath time. You need to *finish what you are doing* and then we'll take a look at your picture schedule." Notice she directs his attention to the schedule. This makes it the schedule "telling" Drew what to do instead of his mom. This decreases the likelihood of Drew being confrontational.

"Okay, Drew. Let's check the schedule." Drew says, "But, mom! I'm almost finished with my picture." Drew's mom looks and sees that he IS almost finished with his picture. Instead of demanding that he stop this minute, or pulling it away in frustration, she sits on the floor with him and admires his work. This is *prudent flexibility*. Drew is feeling pretty good about the positive attention that he is getting from his mom. "Okay, partner! Time to scoot!" She might even say, "I'll finish picking this stuff up, while you go check your schedule." *This is a diversion tactic, to keep him moving along.*

Drew checks his schedule, and together they go to the bathroom. Drew's mom can feel he is getting more tense. She keeps it light. Maybe she knows that Drew is the kind of boy who doesn't like a lot of talking when he's getting agitated, so she is quiet. She doesn't rush him either. Together they decide on the temperature of the water. She knows that once he's in the water, she can carefully add more hot water if necessary.

Mom: "Okay, Drew, now remember, I'm going to wash your hair in 5 minutes, then you can play in the tub or get out right away."

Drew: "No! I don't want to!"

Mom: "I know you don't" (states fact, does not argue). "We'll hurry up so we can go watch our movie together" (reminds him of reward). Notice that Drew's mom does not ask him if she can wash his hair; she states it as a fact. She knows that if she asks Drew, the answer will be no.

Mom, "Okay Drew, do you want the Pikachu shampoo or the Spiderman shampoo?" (Both of these are special-interest characters that Drew likes.) This is an either/or question that allows Drew to feel he has some control over the situation, which leads to less resistance.

Drew chooses his shampoo. Mom provides him with a dry washcloth to cover his eyes and carefully washes his hair.

Drew: "Mom! I don't like it!"

Mom: "I know. Almost done and then we can watch our movie" (reminds him of reward).

Drew's mom counts the number of rinses it takes (countdown), but she is slow and deliberate; she doesn't panic and therefore he is less panicked as well.

As expected, as soon as Drew exits the tub after his bath, he immediately gets his reward. This is the case even if Drew is "mostly" cooperative. That is, even if he was rumbling, if he was able to pull it together, it merits a reward because he worked hard to earn it.

Note: Drew and his mom are not going to an event; bathing IS the event. This eliminates the need to rush and the accompanying stress.

My five-year-old daughter Kaede just popped by and asked, "What are you writing about, Mama?" To which I replied, "Taking baths. Some kids don't like to take them. And SOME kids," I said as I gently poked a teasing finger at her, "don't like to have their hair washed!" She said smugly in a sing-song voice, "You can't wash my hair!" I asked, "Why not?" Big smile, "Because I dumped all the shampoo down the sink!" And with that she brushed her hands together like a

job well done and went off to play. Serves me right for writing about bathing while my daughter is playing in the bathroom!

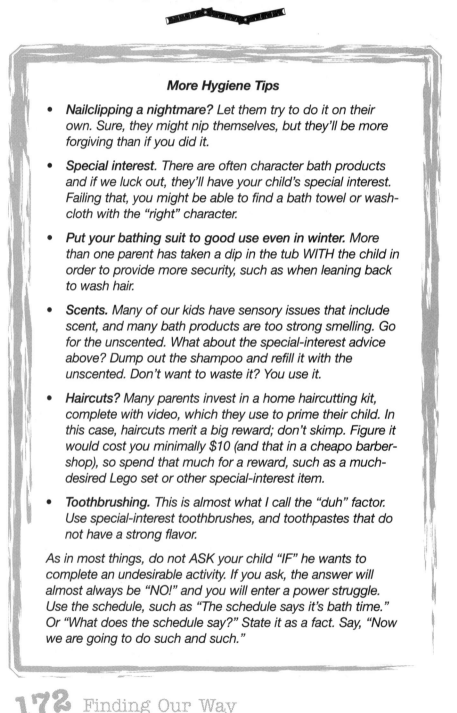

More Hygiene Tips

- **Nailclipping a nightmare?** *Let them try to do it on their own. Sure, they might nip themselves, but they'll be more forgiving than if you did it.*

- **Special interest.** *There are often character bath products and if we luck out, they'll have your child's special interest. Failing that, you might be able to find a bath towel or wash-cloth with the "right" character.*

- **Put your bathing suit to good use even in winter.** *More than one parent has taken a dip in the tub WITH the child in order to provide more security, such as when leaning back to wash hair.*

- **Scents.** *Many of our kids have sensory issues that include scent, and many bath products are too strong smelling. Go for the unscented. What about the special-interest advice above? Dump out the shampoo and refill it with the unscented. Don't want to waste it? You use it.*

- **Haircuts?** *Many parents invest in a home haircutting kit, complete with video, which they use to prime their child. In this case, haircuts merit a big reward; don't skimp. Figure it would cost you minimally $10 (and that in a cheapo barber-shop), so spend that much for a reward, such as a much-desired Lego set or other special-interest item.*

- **Toothbrushing.** *This is almost what I call the "duh" factor. Use special-interest toothbrushes, and toothpastes that do not have a strong flavor.*

As in most things, do not ASK your child "IF" he wants to complete an undesirable activity. If you ask, the answer will almost always be "NO!" and you will enter a power struggle. Use the schedule, such as "The schedule says it's bath time." Or "What does the schedule say?" State it as a fact. Say, "Now we are going to do such and such."

Clothing

Shoes are a big issue. I thought I was a smarty pants and bought slip-on shoes through the mail that looked remarkably similar to what the boys wore last year. This is what happened when the package arrived.

Call first child in to try on school shoes. This is a very unhappy boy. He does not want to wear shoes right now, but I convince him. He tries to put on one shoe, but it turns out the foot opening is not stretchy enough. He insists they will NOT go on. It's difficult, but I manage to get one on him. He hollers, "It hurts! It hurts!" I take it off and feel around inside. Pull out minuscule piece of tissue paper I'd missed. After I have squeezed it back onto his foot, he again hollers, "It hurts! It hurts!" Take off shoe. I try them on myself (same size). I can't feel anything wrong. Crying child insists he will never wear the shoes EVER. Send child off to play.

Call for second child. Pretty much repeat of the previous story. Only, at the end, the third child (who does not yet attend school) comes into the room and begins crying because she did not get new shoes.

Send all children outside to play (barefoot). Put school shoes back in box. Fill out return slip and affix return label. Fix myself a cup of tea, wondering if my children can attend school in their socks. (Ultimately they wore Birkies.)

If the above story sounds like your life, you have clearly dealt with the joy of shopping for clothes and shoes for your child with Asperger Syndrome. Adverse reactions to clothing is often one of the signs that parents notice long before their children are diagnosed. For example, a baby howls for an unknown reason until mom realizes he is calm when dressed in 100% cotton. A toddler screams until he's able to pull off his shoes. A preschooler has a meltdown and refuses to wear new clothes, preferring well-broken-in hand-me-downs, even holey ones (they're air-conditioned, Mom!). There are a lot of naked AS children under the age of five running around the house behind closed drapes – and a few much older children as well. And many puzzled parents will eventually understand what you have already figured out: Sensory issues play a major role in clothing for our AS children.

Here are some tips to add to your own repertoire.

Second-Hand Clothes

An increasing number of stores carry high-quality used children's clothing. Something that is well broken-in is less likely to bother kids like ours. The drawback is the time and effort it takes to dig through the duds to find just the right thing. Some parents actually find shopping an enjoyable break from home while their spouse watches the kids. The upside is that second-hand clothes are considerably cheaper than new ones.

Softly Made Clothing

High-quality clothing made from untreated or whole-fiber cotton is more expensive, but it is also well worth the cost for several reasons.

* It's better to buy two or three outfits that your child will insist on wearing repeatedly than to buy a closet full of clothes he will scream about and refuse to wear.

* These types of clothes usually do not change style very often. Our AS kids often prefer the same textures, the same fit and style. You will be assured of the consistency of the items you purchase.

* This type of clothing lasts longer because it is better made.

* When your child outgrows these more expensive items of clothing, if he has worn them holey, it was money well spent. If not, they will easily be snapped up by your local children's resale shop.

New Clothes

If you can't afford the higher-quality stuff, go for the in-between and wash the clothes several times before they are worn the first time. Remove the tags immediately. Scissors are handy, but they can leave just enough of the tag so that it scratches. Try a stitch ripper or an exacto knife to avoid those chewed-looking holes at the back of the neck of the shirts.

Catalogue Shopping

Experienced "Mall Hell"? Try mail order. Although you may occasionally have to return items, mail order companies have made it increasingly easier to do. Once you have figured out what works well for your child, you can order the same item in every color and you're set. If you're lucky, the next year, you can just order the same thing in the next size up. Recommendations: HannaAndersson.com, Landsend.com, Gap.com

Shoes and Socks

As suggested earlier, shoes can be a challenge for children with Asperger Syndrome, who often have poor muscle tone and problems with gross-motor skills that make walking, running and just keeping their balance difficult. Well-fitting shoes would be ideal. Unfortunately, for many of our kids "well-fitting" translates as "so tight I cannot wear them without screaming." In addition, their fine-motor skill problems make it difficult for them to learn to tie shoes.

Many families solve the problems by providing slip-on or Velcro-closure shoes. Fleecy boots are a recent, and increasingly less expensive, alternative, but make sure they are made with real cotton or wool fleece; poly is scratchy or hot for many of our kids. As for socks, get tube (no seams) or no socks at all! Yes, it means their shoes will smell, but here's a little tip: Use deodorizing foot powder.

Mismatched Misadventures

Our oldest son had a foot-flapping problem. The sound coming from the kitchen was slap, slap, slap across the floor. It drove us crazy (okay, it drove ME crazy). Shortly after he was diagnosed with

Asperger Syndrome, I read on an online board that some AS parents thought Birkenstock sandals helped their kids' feet. I'd been a cheapskate up until that point, but for better or worse, the diagnosis seemed to break that habit. My husband was out of town for a week on business and I was going a little stir crazy, so I thought it would be a good time to get out of the house and take the kids downtown to buy Birkies.

I packed up the (then) baby, stroller, water and snacks, too distracted to take note of what my son Tom was wearing. We hardly ever left the house at the time, so it never occurred to me to check. I drove 30 miles to downtown, and upon arrival I unpacked everything in reverse order. Not until then did I notice what fashion combination Tom had dreamt up. He'd put on his little brother's fleece pants, which came to just below his knees (it was July and almost 80 degrees). On his feet he wore two left shoes – a flip-flop and a rubber boot! I groaned, too late to do anything about it. We walked the two blocks to the Birkenstock store and though they might have wondered about my son's choice of footwear, no one said a word. I'm sure the fact that I dropped $150 on shoes (three pairs) probably helped.

As I started the drive home, I reminded myself to pay more attention to what the kids were wearing before leaving the farm the next time. Just then I caught a glimpse of myself in the rearview mirror. I had drips of purple paint in my hair.

At the time I hadn't been sleeping and had been systematically painting our house at night room by room. If you are awake at 3:00 a.m. painting your laundry room purple, you know you have been afflicted by "My child has just been diagnosed and I feel completely helpless" disorder. Paint is cheap therapy. And I needed all the cheap therapy I could get – after all, I had medical co-payments ... and Birkenstocks to pay for.

Apparently the drawback to lack of sleep and paint fumes is that you forget to check what your children are wearing or what your own hair looks like before leaving the house. But perhaps the other side effect is that you don't care!

Tools for Good, Clean Fun!
Family Sensory Activities

What is sensory integration? It sounds like one of those suspiciously made up things that will cost you a lot of money and reap some vague result. Quite honestly, when I first took my son to occupational therapy to work on sensory integration, I didn't quite understand what it was, only that it was something I was supposed to do. But as it turns out, it's not only a real therapy, it reaps real results!

Many of our kids have intense sensory needs. They may be over- or understimulated by their environment and unable to process the input they receive. Providing tools to help their brains and bodies understand the world through play can cross over into almost every aspect of their lives. After all, the environment is all around you; it touches every one of your senses. If you can understand and respond to it correctly, then you know where you fit in.

Therapeutic sensory activities at home are no substitute for occupational therapy, but it can enhance our daily lives. Here is a list of such activities. It may seem too cumbersome to do in your already busy life, but you can try just one or two; you'll find something you might want to repeat over and over because you enjoy it so much. Or give the suggestion to your child and provide support the first time. If he likes it, encourage him to continue doing it.

Too many activities with children are overplanned and overmanaged these days. Provide a supportive and creative environment, and your child will blossom on his own. Remember, a little mess is part of the deal, but it's well worth the price. All of these are good old-fashioned fun/therapy.

Jumping on the Bed

Who says jumping on the bed is not allowed? I want to know why somebody made that rule up. I recommend putting the mattress on the floor to prevent falls. Jumping is good for the vestibular system. And if your child enjoys spinning, it's also a convenient crash pad.

Water

Many of our kids have trouble bathing because of the feel of the water. Help desensitize them without immersion by letting them splash around in the sink. Pull a chair up, lay a couple of towels on the floor to catch the overflow. Then leave a few plastic dishes they can't harm and let the water run a while. Okay, this may not be environmentally friendly, but it's kid friendly! You might even find that the kids unexpectedly start "really" doing the dishes and enjoying it!

If you live in an area where water isn't rationed, let the kids splash around with the hose on the lawn or "wash" the car (you'll probably either need to help or touch it up afterward). Let the children spray you a little, but don't spray them except maybe the tiniest little bit – toes are a good place to aim for. Using various sponges can change the sensory experience: a bumpy sea sponge, a soft chamois, etc.

Dealing with Picky Appetites

Do your kids have picky appetites? If you read the *Food Wars* section earlier, then you're with the rest of us on that. One way we've found to introduce the sight and smell of new foods, vegetables, for example, is for our kids to grow them (you don't need a large space, a single container will do). It doesn't mean that your children will actually eat broccoli, but it does help them get used to the idea of it being on the table without causing them to gag. Also, knowing they aren't going to be forced to eat something makes it less scary. Let them touch whatever it is they have grown, wash it and then make a big deal about how great it is and how much you are enjoying it. They might just try it some day. It's also an excellent tactile exercise for our kids. Only good can come from touching soil and making things grow.

Preparing Food

If we let our kids handle food, it decreases their aversion to it some-what because we've sent messages to their brains about what the texture and smells are. It becomes more familiar. Again, this doesn't mean your child will instantly eat whatever food he has handled, but it might pique his interest. Never force a child to eat what he has helped prepare. This will counteract the very sense of trusting food you are trying to teach. Always reassure him (if he seems anxious about it) that he doesn't have to eat it unless he wants to.

Suggested activities include tearing lettuce, slicing fruits and veg-etables (with a butter knife), measuring ingredients and grating cheese. You can also allow children to open cans or operate the microwave under your watchful eyes. They will have a sense of accomplishment, and you'll have taught them some important life skills at the same time.

A Rainy Day in June

Do you know what happens when you mix three boxes of lime, two boxes of lemon and one box of strawberry gelatin in one big bowl? Well, it looks kind of purple-ish, until you put it on your spoon. Then oddly it appears to be army green. What does it taste like? "Indescribable" was the word my children used. And "Inedible" was the second word. I hope our chickens like Jello. Anyway, it won't be firm for, oh say, a month or so. If this day had a title it would be, "What to do with three bored children on a rainy day in June." I've long since exhausted my repertoire of Bingo, Don't Break the Ice and Ants in Your Pants, etc. …

Well, the kids aren't made of sugar. They won't melt in the rain, so ducking between drops we decided to do an experiment to see if the ping-pong catapult can fling eggs. It can! But it didn't toss them as far as we'd like them to go, so next we lobbed them up onto the slanted pump house roof. They rolled down with a satisfying splat. The good thing about rain is that it removed most of the evidence before my husband came home. He doesn't have the same appre-ciation for "scientific experiments" as the mother of this house.

*We also did a "sensory experiment." A popular occupational thera-
py activity is playing with shaving cream in order to give AS kids
sensory input. Well, we had a stroke of brilliance. We put on our
bathing suits and liberally decorated ourselves with spray-whipped
cream in the empty Jacuzzi tub. When everyone was thoroughly
sticky and had satisfactorily licked their (own) fingers and arms
enough, it was time to fill it up with water and add a packet of
Aveeno colloidal oatmeal bath soak. It was like being an oatmeal
cookie dipped in a vat of milk (no calories!).*

*Do you suppose my children will remember this? Will I want them to?
How much do you want to bet they'll tell me about it when I'm old
because I'll have dementia and don't remember it myself? Only it
sounds like such a ridiculous story, I probably won't even believe them.*

Helping with Loud Household Activities

The child who holds his hands over his ears and runs away when you
turn on the vacuum might be interested and less afraid if the vacuum
is in his own hands, under his control. Let him play with it, change
the attachments, try it out. Find things that you don't care about (and
that won't plug up the machine) and make a game of sucking them
up. This also demonstrates what can be safely vacuumed. Eventually
"let" the child vacuum his own room.

Make a game out of washing clothes. Let the child dump in the
detergent or wait for the rinse cycle and put in the fabric softener.
This isn't child labor; it's taking the mystery out of things that frighten
our kids, besides taking some of the drudgery out of it for us! We
like to toss the toasty warm clothes straight from the dryer onto the
kids' laps. They always say, ahhhhh. They've learned to listen for
the buzzer, which used to be a startling noise but now has become
one of happy anticipation.

Piggy in a Blanket

You're never too old to be swaddled. Watch your child carefully
when you do any activity that involves restraining him in any way.

He might get scared if he feels as if he is not the one in control. That said, roll the kid in a blanket, most of our kids love that pressure – roll, unroll, roll, unroll.

Pillow fights are also good clean fun – an activity for teaching children unexpected touch. Keep it light and let them whallop you in between. Have a good exaggerated fall or crash once in a while; they will be delighted. Another thing you can do with small children is "sandwich," a mini family pile-up, with you the slice of bread on the bottom.

Good-natured, light-hearted physical play is excellent for helping our kids develop trust in how their bodies work and react to unexpected stimuli in a safe environment. The key is to keep it at an even keel. Don't let them get too worked up. If they do, bring it down a notch. It's much easier to slow down an activity you are directly involved in than to holler "Cut it out, you little monsters, you're getting too wild!" from another room. And it's more fun, too.

Falling Stars

All parents have those moments they hope their children forget! And, of course, we have those moments we hope they remember too. We hold on to them in our hearts and we hope they do as well. Our family has many memories and, for whatever reason, they often seem to happen outside on summer evenings. I don't know what it is that makes these moments stand out; maybe the sense of closeness darkness brings. Fond memories include playing "red light/green light" and "Simon Says" out on the lawn by flashlight, camping in the yard six feet from our back door or cooking hot dogs and s'mores by campfire. Perhaps our children will not remember each and every event, but they will sort of meld into an amalgam of happy memories. And yet, there is one summer night that stands out.

It was August and the meteors were falling like snow. We piled up every blanket and comforter we owned, some beneath us like the Princess on the Pea, and many atop to keep us cozy and warm. We cuddled up together, looking up at the night sky searching for meteors. One child initially whined; he wanted to go inside and play computer. Another was so wiggly she kept letting the chilly night air under the blankets, and the third child's head was burrowed in my armpit because he was so overwhelmed by space and distance. My husband, Nobuo, and I wrapped our reassuring arms around them and soon they settled in.

We sang songs, we giggled, and then a discussion ensued that would have made Carl Sagan proud, after one child mistakenly referred to the meteors as "falling stars." "I'm glad they aren't falling stars," our daughter said, "that would make me sad." The armpit dweller worried that the meteors might really be aliens landing, and that was another interesting topic of discussion. Eventually everyone was still, watching the meteors blaze across the sky, our bodies entangled, our hearts warm. I sang softly to them as one by one they drifted off to sleep. We lay in complete silence. My husband and I turned to smile at each other, our eyes shining in the dark. A moment of complete peace.

Teachable Moments

What is a "teachable moment"? It is simply grabbing the moment to teach your child wherever or whenever an opportunity presents itself. It is an unexpected chance to convey an idea or concept. You might not notice these moments as they slip by, but if you are looking for them, they will appear. For example, we don't just consider riding in the car as getting from one place to another. In our family it is a chance to hold our "audience" captive – all of us can learn a little something. One idea is to teach the "hidden curriculum," which are all the unstated rules of society, all the little things our kids miss if we don't tell them. It's an overwhelming task to do this because there are so many, but Brenda Myles and colleagues (*The Hidden Curriculum*, 2004) remind us that if we teach one per day, that adds up to 365 a year. Okay, so maybe we won't remember every day, but here's the thing about our kids. If they enjoy an activity, they'll remind you. Make it fun, and you might find your kids teaching you a few hidden curriculum items as well!

I was talking about the hidden curriculum with my son Tom. His contribution was, "If you burp in someone's face, you should say, 'Excuse me.'" I said, "How about not burping in someone's face at all?" He looked skeptical and he said, "Well, you could TRY not to."

One More Thing ...

This is my son, "Mama! Mama! Mama!" On a scale of one to five, five being "I'm being maimed or murdered," his voice is at 60,000. Sonic boom level. This volume level of his voice tells me two things:

1. *No one is being maimed or murdered because if they were, for example, if one of the other children were hanging upside down by one ankle from the jungle gym unconscious, he would not be this excited and quick to inform me. Therefore:*

2. *He is about to tell me something VERY IMPORTANT such as, "On one episode of Yu-gi-oh, there was this guy, this guy, um, um, who um, um." There is no point in interjecting at this point, although I do give him the three-finger sign that means, "Volume down to level three before my eardrums burst." (Level three is supposed to signal "normal voice," but for Tom "normal voice" equals the thundering echoes of yodelers calling from one mountain to another.) Other than that, no response is required of me because even if I were to speak, he would not hear me. So I just let him talk.*

"There's this guy, this guy, who, who, um, he ..." And then he uses words I do not completely understand, usually something to do with life point attacks (don't ask!). I think I'm pretty smart for sort of knowing what that means, but I'm even smarter because I know not

to comment because whatever I would say is going to be wrong. Because no matter how much I know about Yu-gi-oh, even if I was the Yu-gi-oh world champion, there is no way I could know enough to carry on a two-sided conversation with my son about it. So, my job is just to listen, and I do mean listen because once in a while some Really Important Thing will slip in during the long explanation that is relevant to my life. Such as, "By the way, my sister IS dangling unconscious from the jungle gym." But otherwise I know that when he takes a breath, I have the opportunity to say, "Okay, you can tell me ONE more thing." This will hopefully give him the signal that it is time to conclude his public service announcement and life can once again commence. Bonus points for me if I am quick to interject this "One Thing" pronouncement before the first Very Important Thing. If he is not satisfied, Plan B.

I touch him on the shoulder and say, "You can tell me about it at bedtime," or "in the car on the way to therapy" or whatever is typically a convenient time that day. Then I try to make sure I do it, even if he forgets. This eventually, although not always, works because it's predictable. He knows how it will happen, which is very reassuring for him. He knows to trust that I WILL give him time to talk.

Typically at bedtime I lie in the boys' room and the tag-team conversation goes on. The oldest will launch into an episode of Yu-gi-oh, then I will say, "It's your brother's turn now." Little Brother will think for five minutes and then say, "We had nachos at school today." Then my daughter, who is also participating, will chime in with something like, "I saw a pillbug! And do you know that butterflies come from cocoons?" We go around like this, in what is often a completely disjointed, jumbled eclectic conversation. At other times they add comments to the subject their sibling has brought up. Which is, sort of, an actual conversation. Either way, it's surprisingly interesting and fun, especially if I indulge myself and take a turn. I have to admit I'm a little guilty of letting this go on longer than I should because I find it so thoroughly enjoyable.

And then I finally say, "Okay, everyone can tell me ONE MORE THING." I listen, we say our prayers, I tuck them in – and if all goes well – I breathe an enormous sigh of relief!

Epilogue

Trevor's Family

At the beginning of the book we met Trevor and his family as they experienced a series of painful difficulties when attending a community potluck at the park. A year has passed and Trevor has been diagnosed with Asperger Syndrome in the meantime. His parents have found professional support, read books and learned to use tools to help Trevor adjust to a variety of situations. Through their journey they have also met other families like theirs and developed relationships. This is the story of the next time they went to the park.

A Day to Remember (in a Good Way!)

Trevor and his parents went to the park to meet some friends from their Asperger Parent support group. While the children played in the sandbox, and some of them on the equipment, the adults stayed close at hand, ready to step in when necessary. Trevor's dad helped his son up to the top of the jungle gym carefully, talking him through it and giving him lots of physical support. Although Trevor was initially reluctant, he was excited when he got to the top and felt proud of himself. Other parents smiled appreciatively because they understood the significance of this accomplishment.

One small incident occurred. Two children began to bicker over a toy, but the dad was quick to step between them and divert his son's rumbling behavior by using the "walk and don't talk" technique he'd read about in the *Difficult Moments* book (Myles & Southwick, 2005). Later when they returned, one parent said to the dad, "Hey, that was a good strategy, where did you learn that?" and the dad promised to loan him the book.

When it was close to lunch time, the parents called out to the children,

"Fifteen minutes until lunch!" Then "Five Minutes until lunch!" – giving all the children and their families time to transition from play-time to meal-time. It wasn't as crowded as the community potluck the year before, and everyone was respectful of personal space. However, when one child was accidentally bumped, lost his balance and fell into a lady ahead of him, the lady smiled knowingly at his parents.

When it was Trevor and his parents' turn at the table, there were lots of things he could eat because no one brought a salad or a casserole. His mom said, "Look Trevor, I brought two of your favorite foods and I set some aside just in case!" His mom's best friend knew that Trevor liked strawberry pie. She slipped a piece onto his plate that she'd been holding back and whispered, "I made another whole pie you can take home when you leave." Trevor's mom and her friend smiled at each other.

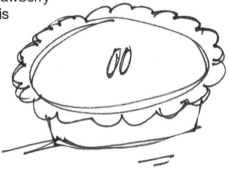

One child had a meltdown; he was having an off day. But no one looked on unkindly or interfered. Instead they cast eyes of sympathy and support toward the parents and compassion for the child. Later when things calmed down, the mom, whose child was newly diagnosed, looked pretty upset. Trevor's mom went over and gave her a hug, offered her some support and said, "I know just how it feels." And she does!

Families left early if their kids were frayed, but the entire event didn't last too long anyway. These parents know to "keep it short to ensure success." As Trevor and his parents drove home that day, they smiled at each other. It was a good day!

Okay, does this sound like fantasy land to you? It's not; it happens almost every weekend somewhere. Families like ours accept and support each other. Parents use and share tools. Children's needs are taken into consideration. Wouldn't it be a better world if ALL family gatherings, Asperger group or not, were this supportive? Do you have this kind of community? No? Then create one. You have the eyes of understanding, the right tools for effectively parenting your Asperger Child, and you can build your community of support. Now, it's up to you.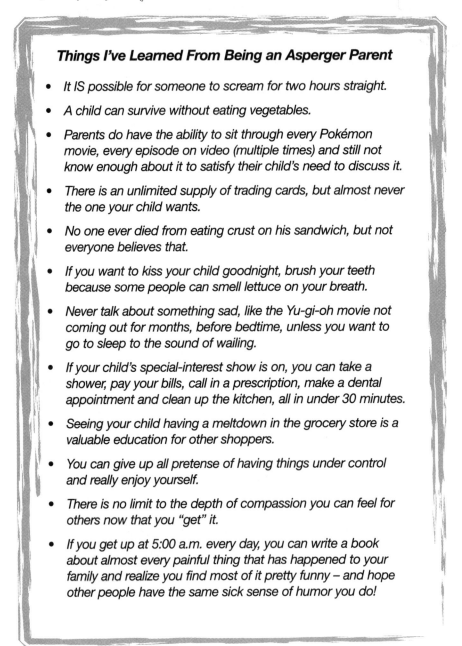

Things I've Learned From Being an Asperger Parent

- *It IS possible for someone to scream for two hours straight.*

- *A child can survive without eating vegetables.*

- *Parents do have the ability to sit through every Pokémon movie, every episode on video (multiple times) and still not know enough about it to satisfy their child's need to discuss it.*

- *There is an unlimited supply of trading cards, but almost never the one your child wants.*

- *No one ever died from eating crust on his sandwich, but not everyone believes that.*

- *If you want to kiss your child goodnight, brush your teeth because some people can smell lettuce on your breath.*

- *Never talk about something sad, like the Yu-gi-oh movie not coming out for months, before bedtime, unless you want to go to sleep to the sound of wailing.*

- *If your child's special-interest show is on, you can take a shower, pay your bills, call in a prescription, make a dental appointment and clean up the kitchen, all in under 30 minutes.*

- *Seeing your child having a meltdown in the grocery store is a valuable education for other shoppers.*

- *You can give up all pretense of having things under control and really enjoy yourself.*

- *There is no limit to the depth of compassion you can feel for others now that you "get" it.*

- *If you get up at 5:00 a.m. every day, you can write a book about almost every painful thing that has happened to your family and realize you find most of it pretty funny – and hope other people have the same sick sense of humor you do!*

References

American Psychiatric Association. (2000). *Diagnostic and statistical manual of mental disorders* (4th ed., text revision). Washington, DC: Author.

Buron, K.D. (2003). *When my autism gets too big! A relaxation book for children with autism spectrum disorders*. Shawnee Mission, KS: Autism Asperger Publishing Company.

Buron, K.D., & Curtis, M. (2003). *The incredible 5-point scale: Assisting students with autism spectrum disorders*. Shawnee Mission, KS: Autism Asperger Publishing Company.

Center on Addiction and Substance Abuse, Columbia University. (2004). *The importance of family dinners*. New York: Author.

Faherty, C. (2000). *What does it mean to me? A workbook explaining self-awareness and life lessons to the child or youth with high functioning autism or Asperger's*. Arlington, TX: Future Horizons.

Greene, R. (2001). *The explosive child: A new approach for understanding and parenting easily frustrated, chronically inflexible children*. New York: Harper Collins.

Kranowitz, C.S. (1998). *The out-of-sync child: Recognizing and coping with sensory integration dysfunction.* New York: Perigee Books.

Myles, B. S., Cook, K. T., Miller, N. E. Rinner, L., & Robbins, L. (2000). *Asperger Syndrome and sensory issues: Practical solutions for making sense of the world.* Shawnee Mission, KS: Autism Asperger Publishing Company.

Myles, B. S., & Savner, J. L. (2000). *Making visual supports work in the home and community. Strategies for individuals with autism and Asperger Syndrome*. Shawnee Mission, KS: Autism Asperger Publishing Company.

Myles, B. S., Simpson, R. L., & Bock, S. (1999). *Asperger Syndrome Diagnostic Scale.* Austin, TX: Pro-Ed.

Myles, B. S., & Southwick, J. (2005) *Asperger syndrome and difficult moments: Practical solutions for tantrums, rage and meltdowns*. Shawnee Mission, KS: Autism Asperger Publishing Company.

Myles, B. S., Troutman, M. L., & Schelvan, R. L. (2004). *The hidden curriculum: Practical solutions for understanding unstated rules in social situations*. Shawnee Mission, KS: Autism Asperger Publishing Company.

Sears, W. (1999). *Nighttime parenting: How to get your baby and child to sleep*. Shaumberg, IL: La Leche League International.

Skinner, B.F. (1953). *Science and human behavior*. New York: Macmillan.

Thevenin, T. (1987). *The family bed: An age-old concept in child rearing*. New York: Berkley Publishing Group.

Family Resources

Buron, K. D., & Curtis, M. (2003). *The incredible 5-point scale: Assisting students with autism spectrum disorders in understanding social interactions and controlling their emotional responses.* Shawnee Mission, KS: Autism Asperger Publishing Company.

Cardon, T. A. (2004). *Let's talk emotions.* Shawnee Mission, KS: Autism Asperger Publishing Company.

Elliot, L. B. (2002). *Embarrassed often, ashamed never: Quips and short stories from one family's ongoing adventure with Asperger Syndrome and autism.* Shawnee Mission, KS: Autism Asperger Publishing Company.

Greene, R. (2001). *The explosive child: A new approach for understanding and parenting easily frustrated, chronically inflexible children.* New York: Harper Collins.

Kranowitz, C. S. (1998). *The out-of-sync child: Recognizing and coping with sensory integration dysfunction.* New York: Perigee Books.

Lieberman, L. A. (2005). *A "stranger" among us: Hiring in-home support for a child with autism spectrum disorders or other neurological differences.* Shawnee Mission, KS: Autism Asperger Publishing Company.

McAffee, J. (2002). *Navigating the social world: A curriculum for individuals with Asperger's Syndrome, high functioning autism, and related disorders.* Arlington, TX: Future Horizons.

Moore, S. T. (2002). *Asperger syndrome and the elementary school experience: Practical solutions for academic and social difficulties.* Shawnee Mission, KS: Autism Asperger Publishing Company.

Myles, B. S., & Adreon, D. (2001). *Asperger Syndrome and adolescence: Practical solutions for school success.* Shawnee Mission, KS: Autism Asperger Publishing Company.

Myles, B. S., Cook, K. T., Miller, N. E. Rinner, L., & Robbins, L. (2000). *Asperger Syndrome and sensory issues: Practical solutions for making sense of the world*. Shawnee Mission, KS: Autism Asperger Publishing Company.

Myles, B. S., & Savner, J. L. (2000). *Making visual supports work in the home and community. Strategies for individuals with autism and Asperger Syndrome.* Shawnee Mission, KS: Autism Asperger Publishing Company.

Myles, B. S., Simpson, R. L., & Bock, S. (1999). *Asperger Syndrome Diagnostic Scale*. Austin, TX: Pro-Ed.

Myles, B. S., & Southwick, J. (2005). *Asperger Syndrome and difficult moments: Practical solutions for tantrums, rage and meltdowns*. Shawnee Mission, KS: Autism Asperger Publishing Company.

Myles, B. S., Troutman, M. L., & Schelvan, R. L. (2004). *The hidden curriculum: Practical solutions for understanding unstated rules in social situations*. Shawnee Mission, KS: Autism Asperger Publishing Company.

For Children with Asperger Syndrome:

Buron, K.D. (2004). *When my autism gets too big! A relaxation book for children with autism spectrum disorders*. Shawnee Mission, KS: Autism Asperger Publishing Company.

Faherty, C. (2000). *Asperger's – What does it mean to me? A workbook explaining self-awareness and life lessons to the child or youth with high-functioning autism or asperger's.* Arlington, TX: Future Horizons.

Gagnon, E., & Myles, B. S. (1999). *This is Asperger Syndrome*. Shawnee Mission, KS: Autism Asperger Publishing Company.

Myles, H. M. (2002) *Practical solutions for everyday challenges for children with Asperger Syndrome*. Shawnee Mission, KS: Autism Asperger Publishing Company.

For Siblings:

Bleach, F. (2002). *Everybody is different – A book for young people who have brothers or sisters with autism*. Shawnee Mission, KS: Autism Asperger Publishing Company.

Feiges, L., & Weiss, M. J. (2004). *Sibling stories: Reflections on life with a brother or sister on the autism spectrum.* Shawnee Mission, KS: Autism Asperger Publishing Company.

Harris, S. L. (1994). *Siblings of children with autism: A guide for families.* Bethesda, MD: Woodbine House.

DVD:

Buron, K. D., & Curtis, M. (2005). *The incredible 5-point scale: Assisting students in understanding social interactions and controlling their emotional responses.* Shawnee Mission, KS: Autism Asperger Publishing Company.

Myles, B. S. (2005). *The hidden curriculum: Teaching what is meaningful.* Shawnee Mission, KS: Autism Asperger Publishing Company.

Myles, B. S. (2005). *Difficult moments for children and youth with autism spectrum disorders.* Shawnee Mission, KS: Autism Asperger Publishing Company.

Websites:

Maap Services, Inc.
www.maapservices.org

Autism Society of America
www.autism-society.org

O.A.S.I.S. Online Asperger Syndrome Information and Support
www.udel.edu/bkirby/asperger

Center for Collaborative Problem Solving
www.explosivechild.com

Gluten-Free Cassein-Free Diet information
www.gfcfdiet.com

Custom-made visual supports and schedules (some free!)
www.Do2Learn.com

Read AAPC's Entire Practical Solutions Series